GiveBack to Algeria

Honouring Our Legacy, Building Our Future

Building Tomorrow, Today

By Toufik Bakhti

Contents

Historical Overview

The journey to Algeria's independence is a powerful narrative of resilience, sacrifice, and unyielding determination. Reflecting on our nation's history, we recognise that the freedoms and opportunities we enjoy today were secured through the immense efforts of those who came before us. Our fathers, grandfathers, and countless others dedicated their lives to the struggle for independence, exemplifying their unwavering commitment to Algeria.

Early Resistance Against French Colonisation (1830-1954)

The fight for Algerian independence did not begin in 1954; it has deep roots going back to the initial French invasion in 1830. From the outset, the Algerian people fiercely resisted French colonisation.

1.   Abdelkader's Resistance (1832-1847): Emir Abdelkader led one of the earliest and most significant uprisings against French rule. His leadership and military prowess enabled him to unify various tribes and establish a substantial resistance movement that held off the French forces for several years before his eventual capture and exile.

2.   Bou Baghla and Lalla Fatma N'Soumer (1851-1857): Bou Baghla, along with the iconic female leader Lalla Fatma N'Soumer, led a notable resistance in the Kabylie region. Their efforts inspired widespread support and demonstrated the ongoing opposition to French control.

3.   Mokrani Revolt (1871): Following years of oppressive policies and land confiscations by the French, Sheikh El Mokrani led a major rebellion in 1871. This uprising saw widespread participation and was a powerful statement of the continued resistance to colonial rule, even though it was eventually suppressed.

4.   Cheikh Bouamama (1881-1908): Another significant uprising was led by Cheikh Bouamama, a religious and tribal leader, who galvanised support among the tribes of the southwest to fight against the French

colonial forces. His resistance lasted for several decades, highlighting the enduring spirit of opposition among the Algerian people.

5.   1916 Uprising: Amidst World War I, there was a significant uprising in the Aures region led by the Ouled Sidi Sheikh tribe. This revolt was driven by discontent with French recruitment policies and the harsh economic conditions imposed on the local population.

The Rise of Algerian Nationalist Movements and the Association of Algerian Muslim Ulama (1930s-1950s)

In the early 20th century, the struggle for independence began to take a more organised, ideologically driven form, with the emergence of various nationalist movements and the influential role of the Association of Algerian Muslim Ulama.

1. The Emergence of Nationalist Movements: During the 1930s, several political organisations emerged, advocating for the rights and independence of the Algerian people. Notable among these was the North African Star (Étoile Nord-Africaine), founded by Messali Hadj in 1926, which played a crucial role in galvanising nationalist sentiments. This movement laid the groundwork for future political activism and inspired the formation of other nationalist groups.

2. The Role of the Association of Algerian Muslim Ulama: Founded in 1931 by Sheikh Abdelhamid Ben Badis and other prominent scholars, the Association of Algerian Muslim Ulama (Association des Ulama Musulmans Algériens) was a significant cultural and religious movement. The Ulama focused on revitalising Islamic values, promoting Arabic language and education, and preserving Algerian identity against French colonial assimilation policies. Their motto, "Islam is our religion, Arabic is our language, and Algeria is our homeland," encapsulated their mission.

3. The Algerian People's Party (PPA): In 1937, Messali Hadj transformed the North African Star into the Algerian People's Party (Parti du Peuple Algérien), which sought complete independence from France. The PPA became a leading force in the nationalist movement, advocating for political mobilisation and national consciousness.

4. The Manifesto of the Algerian People (1943): During World War II, Ferhat Abbas, initially a moderate nationalist, issued the "Manifesto of the Algerian People," calling for the recognition of Algerian sovereignty. This

document highlighted the aspirations for self-determination and equal rights, further galvanising nationalist sentiments.

The Fight for Independence (1954-1962)

The resistance against French colonisation took a more organised and militant form in the mid-20th century, culminating in the Algerian War of Independence.

6.   The Setif Massacre (May 8, 1945): The initial spark for resistance in the modern era can be traced back to this tragic event when peaceful demonstrations in Setif, Guelma, and Kherrata were met with violent repression by French forces, resulting in thousands of Algerian deaths. This massacre underscored the deep-seated resentment and desire for independence among the Algerian people.

7.   The Outbreak of the Algerian War (November 1, 1954): This date marks the official beginning of the Algerian War of Independence, launched by the National Liberation Front (FLN). The FLN played a crucial role in organising and leading the resistance against French rule.

8.   The Battle of Algiers (1956-1957): One of the most significant and intense phases of the war, the Battle of Algiers, saw the FLN engage in urban guerrilla warfare in the capital. The French military's heavy-handed response, including the use of torture, drew international condemnation and galvanised global support for the Algerian cause.

9.   The Evian Accords (March 18, 1962): The persistent efforts of the FLN and the indomitable spirit of the Algerian people culminated in the signing of the Evian Accords. These agreements led to a ceasefire and paved the way for Algeria's independence, formally declared on July 5, 1962.

The Spirit of Sacrifice in Algerian Belief

The spirit of sacrifice is one of the highest virtues in Algerian heritage, rooted in a deep belief that the nation is worth every sacrifice. From early resistance to the later struggle for independence, Algerians have consistently demonstrated their willingness to give up everything for the freedom and independence of their country. This spirit was evident not only on the battlefields but also in the daily sacrifices made by people in the face of oppression and injustice.

The sacrifices made by the Algerian people are not merely historical memories; they are an integral part of our national identity. Algerians have learned from their ancestors that sacrificing for the homeland is the noblest act. Every Algerian family carries within its stories of individuals who sacrificed their lives or their personal safety for the vision of a free and independent nation. These stories, passed down from generation to generation, fuel the national spirit and remind the current generations that freedom is not free but the result of immense sacrifices.

Detailed Business Plan for the GiveBack to Algeria Initiative

Note to Readers (Status and Scope)

This book is an updated working version of the GiveBack to Algeria (GBTA) concept. It is intended to inform, invite discussion, and support structured preparation.

GBTA is currently in the preparation phase. At the time of writing, it has not yet been formally registered in Algeria. The legal set-up, governance bodies, and operating processes described here represent the proposed model.

Proposed structure:

• A national non-profit association (under Algerian Law 12-06) as the guardian of the public interest and the owner of the initiative.

• A wholly-owned operating company ("Al Amana Development") as the commercial delivery arm to implement projects professionally.

National scope:

• The initiative is designed to operate across all 69 wilayas, with projects prioritised by need, feasibility, and measurable impact.

Funding reference in this book:

• The model is often illustrated using a €25/month reference contribution; the detailed calculation is provided in the Objectives section.

Integrity and cooperation note:

• This book includes a proposed set of mandatory legal safeguards (mission lock, non-distribution, audited reporting, procurement and conflict-of-interest controls) to protect the initiative and the public interest.

• GBTA is designed to complement public bodies through lawful, transparent cooperation (for example, MoUs and project-specific agreements), while remaining citizen-led and non-partisan.

• Qualified legal professionals in Algeria must validate final legal wording and compliance requirements before registration and launch.

Executive Summary

GiveBack to Algeria (GBTA) is a citizen-led, community-owned development initiative designed to channel the energy of Algerians at home and abroad into a transparent, long-term programme of nation-building.

The initiative proposes a governance model that protects the public interest through a non-profit association while enabling professional execution through a wholly owned operating company. All surpluses are intended to be reinvested into further projects — not distributed to individuals.

In practical terms, GBTA aims to launch income-generating projects that can fund broader social and economic impact, while creating jobs, strengthening local economies, and improving quality of life across all 69 wilayas.

This book uses a simple reference contribution of €25/month and outlines a potential 7.5-year mobilisation target of €3.375 billion, subject to legal registration and a formal public launch.

What makes GBTA different:

• Community funding at scale, with transparent reporting and independent oversight.

• A reinvestment model that builds assets and funds future projects sustainably.

• A nationwide approach, ensuring development benefits extend beyond major cities.

• A focus on practical, measurable outcomes: jobs, services, infrastructure, and dignity.

Why GiveBack to Algeria? (The Case for a Citizen-Led Development Engine)

Algeria has immense potential: a young population, abundant resources, talented people at home and across the diaspora, and a powerful national identity. Yet many families still face limited job opportunities, uneven local development, and costly inefficiencies in everyday services and supply chains.

GiveBack to Algeria (GBTA) exists to bridge that gap through an organised, transparent, citizen-led vehicle that can fund and deliver productive projects, then reinvest the surplus into further development across all 69 wilayas.

What GBTA changes is not only what gets built, but how it gets built:

• From fragmented goodwill to structured mobilisation: a trustworthy framework that people can understand and scrutinise.

• From one-off donations to sustainable reinvestment: productive projects that generate revenue and grow impact over time.

• From low trust to high accountability: clear decision rights, independent oversight, audited accounts, procurement rules, and conflict-of-interest controls.

• From selective delivery to nationwide inclusion: projects designed to benefit people in every wilaya, not only major cities.

GBTA is not a substitute for the state. It is a complementary citizen-led platform that helps convert public goodwill into structured, measurable development.

Vision and mission

Vision

A modern, productive and united Algeria — where every citizen, in every wilaya, has fair access to opportunity, quality services, and a dignified standard of living.

Mission

To unite Algerians worldwide in a transparent, accountable institutional framework that funds and delivers sustainable development projects across all 69 wilayas, with every surplus reinvested for the public good.

What success looks like:

• Sustainable job creation and skills development for youth and women.

• Strong local economies in each wilaya, supported by reliable logistics and services.

• Modern, efficient infrastructure that improves daily life and enables growth.

• Better access to education, healthcare, and community facilities.

• Cultural pride and social cohesion are strengthened through shared national progress.

Core Values

Integrity: We act in the public interest, with zero tolerance for corruption or personal gain.

Transparency and Accountability: We publish clear information, welcome scrutiny, and accept an independent audit.

Professionalism: Projects are prepared and executed to high standards, based on competence and evidence.

Inclusivity: The initiative belongs to Algerians everywhere — men and women, inside and outside the country.

Sustainability: We prioritise long-term impact, environmental responsibility, and reinvestment.

Local Empowerment: Communities should benefit, contribute, and have a voice in shaping local priorities.

Governance and Operating Model

GBTA is designed to protect the public interest while delivering projects professionally. The model separates stewardship (the Association) from delivery (Al Amana Development), with apparent oversight and transparent reporting.

Two-entity model (proposed):
• The GBTA National Association (under Algerian Law 12-06): guardian of the public interest; sets strategy and standards; approves the national programme across the 69 wilayas; oversees transparency and independent audit.
• Al Amana Development (wholly owned operating company): the commercial delivery arm mandated to prepare, build, operate and scale projects under agreed controls, budgets and performance targets.

Who does what (decision rights):
• The Association decides: strategy, project selection criteria, annual programme priorities, budget envelopes, appointment/oversight of the operating company board, approval of audited accounts, and publication of public reports.
• Al Amana decides: delivery plans, recruitment, procurement and supplier management (within approved policies), operations, and day-to-day performance management of projects.
• Advisory structures (non-executive): provide independent technical review (legal, finance, engineering, health, education, procurement, HR, IT, impact) and challenge assumptions before projects are approved.

Minimum governance committees (recommended):
• Audit, Ethics and Compliance Committee: conflict-of-interest register, internal controls, and liaison with external auditors.
• Finance and Risk Committee: treasury discipline, financial policies, risk register, and stress-testing of assumptions.
• Projects and Investment Committee: reviews feasibility studies and Project Charters; recommends go/no-go decisions and budget allocations.

Project lifecycle (standard method):
1) Idea intake: needs identified locally in each wilaya (citizens, experts, partners) using a simple submission and screening process.
2) Screening: alignment with GBTA objectives, initial feasibility, and prioritisation.

3) Feasibility and business case: demand analysis, costs, legal checks, staffing plan, risks, and measurable outcomes.

4) Approval: the Association approves a Project Charter (scope, budget, timeline, KPIs, governance, and procurement route).

5) Delivery and operations: Al Amana implements and operates, with regular reporting against KPIs and agreed controls.

6) Monitoring, learning and audit: performance dashboards, impact metrics, post-implementation reviews, and independent audit.

Transparency and safeguards (non-negotiables):

• Procurement discipline: competitive tendering where appropriate, clear evaluation criteria, and documented decisions.

• Conflict-of-interest controls: declarations, recusal rules, and a published register for senior decision-makers.

• Open reporting: annual report, audited accounts, project-level summaries, procurement transparency, and measurable impact indicators.

• No private profit distribution: surpluses are reinvested into new projects and public benefit.

Note: GBTA is currently in the preparation phase. This governance model describes the intended structure to be formalised upon legal registration and formal launch.

Mandatory Legal Protections and Safeguards (Integrity by Design)

GBTA is designed to operate with legal and institutional protections that safeguard the public interest and minimise the risks that commonly undermine well-intentioned initiatives. These protections are core conditions for legitimacy, trust, and durability.

1) Clear legal architecture (two-entity model)

• A national non-profit Association (under Algerian Law 12-06) as guardian of the mission and owner of the initiative.

• A wholly-owned operating company ("Al Amana Development") as the execution vehicle mandated to implement projects professionally.

2) Mission lock: non-distribution and asset protection

• No private profit distribution to individuals. Surpluses are reinvested in public benefit projects.

• Clear asset protection rules and dissolution provisions to ensure assets remain dedicated to public benefit under lawful conditions.

3) Board independence and conflict-of-interest controls

• Unpaid governance roles, formal declarations, recusals, and a maintained register for senior decision-makers.

4) Financial controls, transparency, and independent audit

• Segregation of duties, dual authorisation for payments, structured budgeting, and annual independent audit with publishable summaries.

5) Procurement integrity

• Competitive selection where appropriate, documented evaluation criteria, and strict controls on related-party transactions.

Important note: This book describes the intended safeguards and governance direction. The final legal wording must be reviewed and validated by qualified legal professionals in Algeria to ensure full compliance and enforceability.

Working Hand-in-Hand with Government Bodies (Cooperation without Compromise)

GBTA is designed to strengthen development outcomes through a citizen-led, transparent platform. This creates opportunities to work constructively with public institutions while maintaining independence, integrity, and non-partisanship.

Principles of cooperation:

• Legality and transparency: cooperation must be lawful, documented, and publicly explainable.

• Operational independence: partnerships do not mean political affiliation or loss of mission control.

• Professional delivery: clear scope, timelines, responsibilities, and reporting.

Practical cooperation routes:

• Memoranda of Understanding (MoUs) to define collaboration frameworks and shared objectives.

• Project-specific agreements for permits facilitation, land access arrangements where lawful, and structured local stakeholder engagement.

• Joint steering groups for pilot projects with clear decision rights and reporting lines.

What public bodies may gain:

• A credible partner able to mobilise additional resources transparently, pilot delivery models, and publish measurable impact.

Call to Join

GBTA is built on a straightforward idea: when millions contribute a little, a nation can make a lot — transparently and sustainably.

How you can help at this stage:

• Read and share this book so more people understand the model and can challenge it constructively.

• Talk to family and friends (men and women) and encourage them to follow and discuss the initiative.

• Offer your expertise — governance, law, finance, engineering, health, education, communications — to strengthen the preparation phase.

• When participation mechanisms are formally launched, pledge your support and use the hashtag #GiveBacktoAlgeria to help reach 1 of 1,500,000.

GiveBack to Algeria – Honouring Our Legacy, Building Our Future.

Objectives

1. Raise €3.375 billion over 7.5 years.
2. Fund and develop diverse projects across all 69 wilayas.
3. Promote sustainable development and economic growth.
4. Strengthen the bond between the Algerian diaspora and their homeland.

Total Funds to Be Raised

- Monthly Contribution per Person: €25
- Number of Contributors: 1,500,000
- Duration: 7.5 years (90 months)

Total Funds Calculation

- Monthly Total: 1,500,000 contributors * €25 = €37,500,000
- Annual Total: €37,500,000 * 12 = €450,000,000
- Total Over 7.5 Years: €37,500,000 * 90 = €3,375,000,000

Yearly Contribution Calculation

- Annual Contribution per Person: €25 * 12 = €300
- Total Annual Contribution from All Contributors: 1,500,000 contributors * €300 = €450,000,000

Budget Allocation

- Administration and Operations: 1.5% (€50,625,000)
- Marketing and Engagement: 0.5% (€16,875,000)
- Project Funding: 98% (€3,307,500,000)

Project Funding Allocation

Breakdown by Project Category

1. Chain of Supermarkets (12.5% of Project Funding)
   - Total Allocation: €413,437,500
   - Estimated Number of Projects: fifty supermarkets
   - Average Cost per Project: €8,268,750

Project Description

The "GiveBack to Algeria" initiative, spearheaded by our chain of supermarkets, embodies a transformative vision for the country's retail landscape. This initiative is crucial in streamlining the distribution network, thereby eliminating the excessive intermediaries that currently inflate costs and diminish efficiencies. By focusing on direct procurement, we aim to bridge the gap between producers and consumers, ensuring that products move swiftly from farms and factories to the shelves of our supermarkets.

One of the key strategies of our initiative is to establish a robust, expansive distribution network. This network is essential for several reasons. Firstly, it reduces the dependency on numerous intermediaries who traditionally take a cut at each stage of the supply chain. By sourcing products directly from farmers and manufacturers, we can significantly reduce costs, ensuring savings are passed on to our customers. This approach not only makes our prices more competitive but also provides producers with a fairer deal, enabling them to sell their goods at better margins.

In Algeria, traditional food markets have long been a cornerstone of daily life, offering a vibrant array of fresh produce, meats, and other essentials. However, these markets often suffer from inefficiencies such as inconsistent supply, variable quality, and fluctuating prices. The modernisation of these markets is imperative to meet the growing demands of a modern consumer base. By integrating the latest technology in stock management, storage, and logistics, our supermarkets can offer a more reliable and consistent shopping experience.

Advanced stock management systems ensure that our shelves are always stocked with fresh products, reducing waste and optimising inventory. Modern storage facilities, equipped with state-of-the-art refrigeration and preservation technologies, help maintain the quality and longevity of perishable goods. Efficient logistics operations, leveraging cutting-edge software for route planning and delivery scheduling, ensure that products are transported quickly and safely from suppliers to stores.

The "GiveBack to Algeria" initiative is not just about improving efficiency and reducing costs; it is also about creating a sustainable and equitable food distribution system. By collaborating closely with local farmers and producers, we foster a sense of community and support the local economy. This initiative is a step towards building a more resilient food supply chain that can withstand market fluctuations and provide stable prices for consumers.

Moreover, the modernisation efforts will set new standards for the retail industry in Algeria, encouraging other market players to adopt similar practices. This collective movement towards efficiency and innovation will benefit the entire ecosystem, from producers to consumers.

In conclusion, our supermarket chain's involvement in the "GiveBack to Algeria" initiative is a testament to our commitment to transforming the country's food distribution network. By reducing intermediaries, leveraging modern technology, and supporting local producers, we aim to provide high-quality products at competitive prices, all while fostering sustainable economic growth. This initiative is a crucial step towards a modern, efficient, and equitable retail environment in Algeria.

GiveBack to Algeria: Supermarket Chain Concept

The GiveBack to Algeria initiative aims to support local communities by establishing a chain of supermarkets that cater to diverse shopping needs while promoting local produce and products. The supermarket chain will feature a variety of store types designed to serve communities of different sizes and shopping preferences. Here is an outline of the proposed store formats:

1. HyperMax

Description: HyperMax stores are large hypermarkets that provide a comprehensive range of products, including food, clothing, electronics, and home goods. These stores will serve as one-stop shopping destinations, offering an extensive product range and additional services.

Size and Capacity:

- Average Size: 5,000 to 9,000 square meters
- Product Range: Wide array of groceries, fresh produce, clothing, electronics, furniture, and more.
- Parking Facilities: Large parking areas to accommodate hundreds of vehicles.
- Services: Pharmacies, opticians, photo services, cafes/restaurants, and areas for community events.

Example: A HyperMax store will serve a wide regional area, stocking tens of thousands of product lines to handle large volumes of shoppers and diverse product offerings.

2. SuperMart

Description: SuperMart stores are standard supermarkets that offer a broad selection of groceries and household goods. Typically located in suburban areas and smaller towns, these stores provide a convenient shopping experience for both weekly and bulk purchases.

Size and Capacity:

- Average Size: 1,800 to 4,500 square meters
- Product Range: Comprehensive range of groceries, fresh produce, and household items, with a more limited selection of non-food items compared to HyperMax.
- Parking Facilities: Moderate to large parking areas.
- Services: In-store bakeries, delis, and sections for clothing and household items.

Example: SuperMart stores cater to families and individuals seeking a wide variety of products, offering thousands of items.

3. UrbanFresh

Description: UrbanFresh stores are medium-sized, located in city centres and other urban areas, focusing on convenience and frequent shopping. They are ideal for daily or top-up shopping, providing essential groceries and ready-to-eat meals.

Size and Capacity:

- Average Size: 600 to 1,300 square meters
- Product Range: Groceries, ready-to-eat meals, and everyday essentials.
- Parking Facilities: Limited or no dedicated parking, with street or nearby public parking options.
- Services: Basic services such as cash machines and small in-store bakeries.

Example: UrbanFresh stores will support busy urban lifestyles, offering 5,000 to 10,000 product lines for quick, efficient shopping.

4. QuickShop

Description: QuickShop stores are small convenience stores located in residential and high-traffic areas. Designed for quick and convenient shopping, they offer essential groceries and immediate needs items.

Size and Capacity:

- Average Size: 180 to 450 square meters
- Product Range: Essential groceries, snacks, beverages, and ready-to-eat items.
- Parking Facilities: Limited or no dedicated parking.
- Services: Focused on convenience with self-checkout options.

Example: QuickShop stores offer a compact selection of 3,000 to 7,000 products, ideal for quick top-ups and urgent purchases.

5. Neighbourhood

Description: Neighbourhood stores are smaller neighbourhood convenience stores aimed at providing basic groceries and household essentials at competitive prices. They will be in residential neighbourhoods to serve the daily needs of local communities.

Size and Capacity:

- Average Size: 90 to 250 square meters
- Product Range: Core range of groceries, snacks, and household essentials.
- Parking Facilities: Minimal or on-street parking.
- Services: Basic services focused on convenience, such as bill payments and mobile top-ups.

Example: Neighbourhood stores will carry a limited range of 2,000 to 5,000 products, suitable for quick, everyday shopping.

The GiveBack to Algeria supermarket chain will feature a range of store formats, from large hypermarkets (HyperMax) to small convenience stores (Neighbourhood), ensuring the diverse shopping needs of Algerian communities are met. By promoting local produce and providing essential services, these stores will enhance community engagement and support economic development across Algeria.

Market Research and Planning:

To ensure the supermarket chain's success, comprehensive market research and planning will be conducted. This involves analysing consumer needs, identifying optimal locations, and understanding local market dynamics. Detailed feasibility studies will assess the potential demand and profitability of each supermarket. Strategic partnerships with local producers and suppliers will be established to ensure a steady and diverse supply of goods. Marketing plans will be developed to build brand awareness and attract customers, leveraging both traditional and digital media channels.

2. Chain of Hotels (10% of Project Funding)
    o Total Allocation: €320,625,000
    o Estimated Number of Projects: twenty hotels
    o Average Cost per Project: €16,031,250

Project Description

The "GiveBack to Algeria" initiative is embarking on an ambitious project to create a chain of hotels that will transform Algeria into a premier destination for both local and international tourists. This initiative aims to capitalise on Algeria's vastness and diversity, offering visitors a unique experience that combines luxury with the country's rich cultural heritage.

Algeria, the largest country in Africa and the Arab world, spans an impressive 2.38 million square kilometres. This vast land is home to a population of over forty-three million people. It features a wide array of landscapes, from the pristine Mediterranean coastline to the dramatic Sahara Desert, which covers more than 80% of the country. Algeria's diverse geography also includes the fertile Tell Atlas and the majestic Hoggar Mountains, making it a paradise for nature enthusiasts and adventure seekers.

The need for a robust hotel infrastructure in Algeria is evident. Despite its immense potential, Algeria's tourism sector remains underdeveloped. By establishing a chain of hotels, the "GiveBack to Algeria" initiative seeks to address this gap by providing high-quality accommodations for both domestic and international travellers. This development is crucial for promoting local tourism, creating jobs, and boosting the economy.

Hotel Types and Features

The hotel chain will include a diverse range of accommodation types to meet the varied needs and preferences of travellers:

1. Luxury Hotels:
   o Offer high-end accommodations with extensive amenities, personalised services, and elegant surroundings.
   o Features include fine dining restaurants, spa services, and concierge services.
2. Boutique Hotels:
   o Smaller, stylish hotels with unique decor and a personalised experience, often found in urban locations.
   o Emphasis on individualised service and local culture.
3. Resort Hotels:
   o Located in vacation destinations, providing recreational facilities such as swimming pools, golf courses, and spas.
   o Designed for relaxation and leisure activities.
4. Business Hotels:
   o Cater to business travellers with amenities like conference rooms, Wi-Fi, business centres, and central locations.
   o Focus on convenience and efficiency for corporate guests.
5. Airport Hotels:
   o Situated near airports, offering convenient services for travellers, including shuttle services and early/late check-ins.
   o Ideal for transit passengers and short stays.
6. Suite Hotels:
   o Provide separate living areas and kitchen facilities, ideal for families or long-term stays.
   o Offer a home-like environment with hotel services.
7. Extended Stay Hotels:

- o Designed for long-term guests, offering full kitchens and more home-like amenities.
   - o Suitable for travellers on extended business trips or relocations.
8. Budget Hotels:
   - o Provide basic accommodations at a lower cost, ideal for budget-conscious travellers.
   - o Focus on essential amenities and affordable rates.
9. Eco-Friendly Hotels:
   - o Focus on sustainability and environmentally friendly practices, often using green energy and materials.
   - o Implement eco-friendly practices like solar panels and waste recycling.
10. Hostels:
   - o Offer budget-friendly, shared accommodations, typically with dormitory-style rooms and communal areas.
   - o Popular with backpackers and young travellers.
11. Motels:
   - o Usually located along highways, offering convenient, no-frills lodging with easy access to parking.
   - o Ideal for road trip travellers.
12. Bed and Breakfasts (B&Bs):
   - o Small establishments offering overnight accommodation and breakfast, often in a home-like setting.
   - o Provide a cosy and intimate lodging experience.
13. Spa Hotels:
   - o Feature extensive spa services, wellness treatments, and relaxation amenities.
   - o Focus on health and wellness tourism.
14. Heritage Hotels:
   - o Operate in historic buildings, offering a blend of traditional architecture and modern comforts.
   - o Preserve and promote the cultural heritage of the region.
15. All-Inclusive Hotels:
   - o Offer lodging, meals, drinks, and various activities for one inclusive price.

o   Ideal for travellers seeking a hassle-free vacation experience.

16. Conference/Convention Hotels:
    o   Equipped with large meeting spaces and facilities for conferences and events.
    o   Designed to host large-scale business events and gatherings.

17. Serviced Apartments:
    o   Fully furnished apartments available for short or long-term stays, with hotel-like services.
    o   Offer a balance between residential living and hotel amenities.

18. Boutique Guest Houses:
    o   Smaller, personalised accommodations often with unique decor and a homely feel.
    o   Provide an intimate and charming lodging experience.

19. Villas:
    o   Offer private, standalone accommodations, often luxurious, with extensive amenities and services.
    o   Ideal for travellers seeking privacy and exclusivity.

20. Historic Inns:
    o   Offer accommodations in historic buildings, often with antique furnishings and a historic ambience.
    o   Preserve the historical charm while providing modern comforts.

21. Adventure Hotels:
    o   Cater to adventure seekers, providing access to outdoor activities like hiking, skiing, or diving.
    o   Located in regions known for their natural attractions and outdoor activities.

Each hotel in this chain will reflect the unique cultural and architectural heritage of its region. For instance, hotels in coastal cities like Algiers and Oran will feature Mediterranean-inspired designs. At the same time, those in the desert regions, such as Tamanrasset and Djanet, will showcase traditional Berber architecture. The interior designs will incorporate local crafts, art, and textiles, creating an immersive experience that celebrates Algerian artisanry.

Algerian hospitality is renowned for its warmth and generosity, and this will be a cornerstone of the hotel chain. Guests will be welcomed with traditional ceremonies, enjoy personalised service, and savour authentic Algerian cuisine. From the fragrant spices of a well-prepared couscous to the sweetness of date-filled pastries, the culinary offerings will highlight the country's rich gastronomic traditions.

In addition to providing luxurious accommodations, the hotels will focus on sustainability and community involvement. Each property will implement eco-friendly practices, including energy-efficient technologies and waste-reduction programmes. Moreover, the hotels will actively engage with local communities, offering training and employment opportunities to residents and sourcing products from local suppliers.

The creation of this hotel chain will also showcase Algeria's diverse landscapes to tourists. Visitors can explore the ancient Roman ruins of Timgad and Djemila, both UNESCO World Heritage Sites, and hike through the awe-inspiring Tassili n'Ajjer National Park, known for its prehistoric rock art. The coastal cities offer stunning beaches and vibrant markets, while the Sahara offers unforgettable experiences such as camel treks and stargazing under clear desert skies.

In summary, the "GiveBack to Algeria" initiative's hotel chain will play a pivotal role in showcasing Algeria's beauty and diversity. By providing high-quality, culturally immersive accommodations across the country, this initiative will attract tourists, foster economic growth, and celebrate the unique heritage of each Algerian region. This network of hotels will not only enhance the tourism infrastructure but also embody the spirit of Algerian hospitality, making every visitor's stay memorable and enriching.

Market Research and Planning:

Comprehensive market research will be conducted to identify prime hotel locations, understand target customers' preferences, and analyse the competition. Feasibility studies will assess the potential for tourism growth in selected areas. Collaboration with local tourism boards and international travel agencies will help in promoting the hotels. Detailed business plans will outline the operational strategies, marketing initiatives, and financial projections to ensure sustainable growth and profitability.

3. Chain of Shops for Him and Her (10% of Project Funding)
    o   Total Allocation: €320,625,000
    o   Estimated Number of Projects: 100 shops
    o   Average Cost per Project: €3,206,250

Project Description

The initiative to create a chain of shops for both men and women in Algeria, under the GiveBack to Algeria initiative, is both timely and commendable. Here is a detailed breakdown of the proposed shops for both men and women, emphasising the necessity and the added value of having women-run shops for women:

For Him: El Aneek Chain

4. El Aneek Health & Grooming
    - Description: This shop will offer a variety of health and grooming products specifically for men, including skincare, haircare, shaving essentials, and personal hygiene products.
5. El Aneek Clothing & Accessories
    - Description: A wide range of men's clothing and accessories will be available here, from casual wear to formal attire, along with accessories such as belts, ties, wallets, and watches.
6. El Aneek Fitness & Sports
    - Description: This store will cater to men's fitness and sports needs, providing athletic apparel, gym equipment, sports gear, and nutritional supplements.El Aneek Shoes

- Description: A dedicated shop for men's footwear, offering a variety of styles from casual and formal shoes to sports and outdoor footwear.El Aneek Groom
- Description: El Aneel Groom is a boutique dedicated to providing stylish clothing and accessories for men preparing for their wedding day. The shop offers a wide selection of elegant suits, sophisticated accessories, and traditional Algerian clothing, such as El Bournous, ensuring grooms look their best on their special day.

For Her: El Aneeka Chain

7. El Aneeka Health & Beauty
   - Description: This store will offer a comprehensive range of health and beauty products for women, including skincare, haircare, makeup, and wellness products.
8. El Aneeka Clothing & Accessories
   - Description: Women's clothing and accessories will be the focus here, featuring everything from casual wear to evening gowns, along with accessories like jewellery, handbags, scarves, and hats.
9. El Aneeka Fitness & Sports
   - Description: Catering to women's fitness and sports needs, this store will provide athletic wear, fitness equipment, sports gear, and health supplements.
10. El Aneeka Shoes
    - Description: A specialised shop for women's footwear, offering a wide range of styles from casual and formal to athletic and outdoor shoes.
11. El Aneeka Bride
    - Description: Dedicated to bridal wear and accessories, this shop will provide wedding dresses, bridal accessories, shoes, and services to assist brides-to-be in preparing for their big day.

Importance and Need for These Chains

Addressing Market Gaps: The creation of these chains addresses a significant market gap in Algeria, where demand is growing for specialised shops catering to the unique needs of men and women. These shops will provide high-quality products and services that are often not readily available, ensuring customers have access to a diverse range of goods.

Economic Empowerment: By establishing these chains, the initiative will contribute to local economic development by creating jobs, stimulating business growth, and supporting local suppliers. This, in turn, helps strengthen the economy and improve living standards.

Women-Run Shops for Women: El Aneeka Chain

Empowerment and Inclusivity: The El Aneeka chain of shops will be run by women, for women. This approach is crucial for several reasons:

12. Empowerment: Running these shops provides women with valuable business and leadership opportunities, promoting economic empowerment and gender equality.

13. Inclusivity: Women-run shops can better understand and cater to the specific needs and preferences of female customers, ensuring a more personalised and satisfying shopping experience.

14. Community Support: Female entrepreneurs often reinvest in their communities, fostering a supportive network and driving positive social change.

Implementation Strategy

15. Market Research: Conduct thorough research to understand the target audience's needs and preferences in Algeria.

16. Location Selection: Choose strategic locations for the shops in key cities and towns to maximise reach and accessibility.

17. Brand Development: Develop strong branding for both El Aneek and El Aneeka, focusing on quality, customer satisfaction, and community involvement.

18. Product Sourcing: Source high-quality products from reliable suppliers to ensure a diverse, appealing product range.

19. Marketing and Promotion: Launch a comprehensive campaign to raise awareness of the shops and the GiveBack to Algeria initiative.

20. Customer Experience: Focus on creating a pleasant and seamless shopping experience for customers, with knowledgeable staff and excellent customer service.

21. Community Engagement: Engage with the local community through events, promotions, and partnerships to build a loyal customer base and support the GiveBack to Algeria initiative.

This plan aims to not only provide quality products and services but also to contribute positively to the local economy and community development in Algeria, with a special emphasis on empowering women through entrepreneurship.

Market Research and Planning:

Detailed market research will be conducted to understand the shopping habits and preferences of people in different regions. Feasibility studies will assess the potential demand and identify optimal locations for the shops. Strategic partnerships with local and international suppliers will be established to ensure a diverse product range. Comprehensive business plans will outline marketing strategies, operational workflows, and financial projections to ensure the shops' success and sustainability.

4. Apartment Buildings Across Algeria (20% of Project Funding)
   - Total Allocation: €641,250,000
   - Estimated Number of Projects: 100 apartment buildings
   - Average Cost per Project: €6,412,500

Project Description

GiveBack to Algeria: Building a Brighter Future

In recent years, Algeria has faced significant challenges in providing affordable housing for its growing population. The rising demand for quality living spaces, coupled with economic pressures, has made it increasingly difficult for many Algerian families and key community workers to find suitable homes. Recognising this critical need, the GiveBack to Algeria initiative has launched a transformative project to build apartment blocks to address the housing shortage and support the development of community-based programmes.

Addressing the Need for Affordable Housing

Affordable housing remains a pressing issue in Algeria, particularly for those who play essential roles in our communities. Teachers, healthcare staff, and other vital workers often struggle to secure adequate housing due to long waiting lists for government schemes and the high costs of private rentals. The GiveBack to Algeria initiative seeks to alleviate this burden by constructing modern, affordable apartment blocks specifically designed to house these key members of our society.

These new apartment complexes will not only provide comfortable living conditions but will also be strategically located to ensure easy access to workplaces, schools, and healthcare facilities. By offering affordable rental options, the initiative aims to improve the quality of life for teachers, healthcare professionals, and other community members, enabling them to focus on their essential roles without the added stress of housing insecurity.

Revitalising Algeria: Preserving Heritage through Restoration and Preservation

Algeria's cities are brimming with historical significance, featuring old quarters that tell the story of a vibrant past. However, these treasured neighbourhoods face a pressing challenge: the plots of land where many Algerian families have resided for generations have become too small to accommodate the growing number of children and grandchildren. This spatial constraint is pushing families to sell their ancestral homes and relocate, thereby fragmenting these beloved communities. The GiveBack to Algeria initiative seeks to address this issue by providing a sustainable and aesthetically pleasing solution.

Preserving Cultural Heritage

The GiveBack to Algeria initiative is dedicated to the purchase, restoration, and preservation of old buildings and neighbourhoods in various cities across the country. This initiative aims not only to create additional housing but also to safeguard Algeria's rich cultural heritage and rejuvenate its historic urban landscapes. By acquiring these plots and rebuilding them, the project envisions rows of elegant buildings lining picturesque streets, all adhering to a cohesive architectural design. This approach ensures the preservation of the historical essence and charm of these old quarters while accommodating the modern needs of expanding families.

Revitalising Urban Landscapes

The restoration of historic buildings and neighbourhoods serves a dual purpose. Firstly, it preserves the architectural and cultural heritage for future generations, ensuring that the unique character and history of Algerian cities are not lost. Secondly, it offers the opportunity to create new, affordable housing and community spaces within these restored structures, blending the old with the latest in a way that honours the past while building for the future.

This process involves careful planning and collaboration with local authorities, heritage experts, and community members to ensure that the restoration respects the historical significance of these neighbourhoods while meeting modern living standards. The vision for these new developments includes creating spaces that are not only visually stunning but also comfortable and functional. By maintaining a cohesive architectural style, the initiative aims to ensure that the old quarters retain their historical beauty and elegance. This uniformity will enhance the neighbourhoods' overall aesthetic appeal, making them more attractive to residents and visitors alike.

Creating Sustainable Communities

Sustainability is a cornerstone of the GiveBack to Algeria initiative's restoration efforts. The project prioritises the use of eco-friendly materials and energy-efficient technologies in the restoration process, ensuring that the buildings are not only preserved but also adapted to meet contemporary environmental standards. This approach helps reduce the carbon footprint of the restoration activities and ensures that the buildings are sustainable in the long term.

Additionally, the initiative promotes the inclusion of green spaces, community gardens, and pedestrian-friendly areas within restored neighbourhoods. These elements contribute to residents' overall well-being by providing spaces for recreation, socialisation, and connection with nature.

Fostering Community and Continuity

Recognising the importance of community, the GiveBack to Algeria initiative aims to preserve the social fabric and cultural heritage of the old quarters by preventing the sale of these plots to multiple individuals. This approach preserves the unique identity of these neighbourhoods and fosters a sense of belonging and continuity among residents. Community engagement is central to the restoration and preservation efforts. The initiative actively involves residents in the planning and implementation stages, ensuring their voices are heard and their needs are met. Workshops, meetings, and collaborative projects help build a sense of ownership and pride among community members, fostering a collective commitment to preserving their heritage.

By involving residents in the restoration process, the initiative not only enhances the buildings' cultural and historical value but also strengthens community bonds. This collaborative approach ensures that the restored neighbourhoods remain vibrant, dynamic places where people want to live, work, and play.

The GiveBack to Algeria initiative's commitment to the purchase, restoration, and preservation of old buildings and neighbourhoods underscores the value placed on Algeria's cultural heritage and the well-being of its communities. By addressing the urgent need for affordable housing and providing essential spaces for educational and extracurricular activities, this project is paving the way for a brighter, more inclusive future. Through these efforts, the initiative is creating more than just housing; it is preserving history, revitalising urban landscapes, and building sustainable, engaged communities. As these projects continue to unfold across various cities in Algeria, they promise to leave a legacy of resilience, beauty, and cultural pride.

Creating Spaces for After-School Clubs

Beyond addressing housing needs, the GiveBack to Algeria initiative recognises the importance of fostering educational and extracurricular opportunities for young people. To this end, the new apartment blocks will also include premises dedicated to After School Clubs. These clubs will offer a safe and supportive environment for students to engage in a range of activities, from academic support to sports, arts, and technology programmes.

After-school clubs play a crucial role in the holistic development of children and adolescents. They provide a space for students to learn, grow, and develop new skills outside the traditional classroom. By integrating these facilities into apartment complexes, the initiative ensures that children from all backgrounds have access to high-quality after-school programmes, promoting educational equity and community cohesion.

Supporting Community Development

The GiveBack to Algeria initiative is more than just a housing project; it is a comprehensive approach to community development. By providing affordable housing to essential workers and creating spaces for after-school clubs, the project aims to build stronger, more resilient communities. These efforts will help create a positive cycle of growth and development, empowering residents to contribute to their community's well-being.

Moreover, the presence of after-school clubs within the apartment complexes will encourage a sense of community among residents, fostering interactions and relationships that strengthen social bonds. This integrated approach ensures that the initiative's benefits extend beyond individual residents to the community as a whole.

Market Research and Planning:

Comprehensive market research will be conducted to identify suitable locations for the apartment buildings, understand the housing needs of different communities, and assess the feasibility of each project. Detailed planning will ensure that the buildings are designed to meet modern standards of comfort and sustainability. Community engagement will be a key aspect of the planning process, ensuring that the housing solutions align with residents' needs and preferences.

5. Logistics, Storage, and Distribution Centres (10% of Project Funding)
- o Total Allocation: €320,625,000
- o Estimated Number of Projects: thirty centres
- o Average Cost per Project: €10,687,500

Project Description

GiveBack to Algeria: Streamlining Logistics, Storage, and Distribution

Efficient logistics, storage, and distribution are the backbone of any thriving economy. Recognising this, the "GiveBack to Algeria" initiative has launched a comprehensive project to establish state-of-the-art logistics, storage, and distribution centres across Algeria. This initiative aims to enhance the efficiency and reliability of supply chains, reduce costs, and support local businesses, driving economic growth and improving the quality of life for Algerians.

The Importance of Efficient Logistics

Effective logistics systems are critical for ensuring that goods move smoothly from producers to consumers. They reduce transportation time and costs, minimise waste, and ensure that products are available when and where they are needed. For Algeria, improving logistics infrastructure is particularly important given the country's size and diverse geography, which present unique challenges for transportation and distribution.

Modern Storage Facilities

Modern storage facilities are essential for maintaining the quality and longevity of goods, particularly perishable items. The new centres will be equipped with advanced refrigeration and preservation technologies to ensure that food products, pharmaceuticals, and other sensitive items are stored in optimal conditions. These facilities will also include robust security measures to protect stored goods from theft and damage.

Establishing Efficient Distribution Networks

The establishment of efficient distribution networks will help reduce the dependency on numerous intermediaries, who traditionally take a cut at each stage of the supply chain. By centralising distribution, the initiative can lower costs, reduce delays, and improve delivery reliability. This approach will benefit both producers and consumers, ensuring that products reach their destinations quickly and in good condition.

Supporting Local Businesses

The logistics, storage, and distribution centres will provide critical support to local businesses, tiny and medium-sized enterprises (SMEs) that may lack the resources to manage their logistics efficiently. By offering affordable and reliable logistics services, the initiative will help these businesses expand their reach, reduce operational costs, and increase their competitiveness in the market.

Sustainable Practices

Sustainability is a key focus of the GiveBack to Algeria initiative. The logistics centres will implement eco-friendly practices, such as using energy-efficient technologies, reducing waste, and optimising transportation routes to minimise fuel consumption. These efforts will contribute to a greener economy and help mitigate the environmental impact of logistics operations.

Creating Job Opportunities

The development and operation of logistics, storage, and distribution centres will create numerous job opportunities for Algerians. These jobs will range from construction and facility management to logistics coordination and administrative roles. By providing employment opportunities, the initiative will contribute to economic development and improve living standards for many Algerians.

The GiveBack to Algeria initiative's focus on logistics, storage, and distribution is a vital component of its broader strategy to enhance the country's infrastructure and drive economic growth. By establishing modern, efficient logistics centres, the initiative will support local businesses, reduce costs, and improve the availability and quality of goods across Algeria. This project represents a significant step towards building a more connected, efficient, and sustainable economy.

Market Research and Planning:

Comprehensive market research will be conducted to identify optimal locations for the logistics centres, understand the needs of local businesses, and analyse existing supply chain inefficiencies. Detailed feasibility studies will assess the potential demand and profitability of each centre. Partnerships with regional and international logistics firms will be established to leverage best practices and technologies. Strategic planning will ensure the centres are designed and operated to meet the highest standards of efficiency and sustainability.

6. Library in Each Neighbourhood (12.5% of Project Funding)
    o Total Allocation: €413,437,500
    o Estimated Number of Projects: 270 libraries
    o Average Cost per Project: €1,531,250

Project Description

The Need for and Importance of a Chain of Libraries in Every Neighbourhood: Part of the GiveBack to Algeria Initiative

Libraries have long stood as bastions of knowledge, learning, and community engagement. The GiveBack to Algeria initiative aims to bolster these vital institutions by establishing a chain of libraries in every neighbourhood, thereby fostering a culture of reading and lifelong learning across the nation. This effort is not merely about building physical structures; it is about creating spaces that serve as the heart of the local community, providing countless benefits to individuals and society as a whole.

Libraries as Community Spaces

Libraries are more than just repositories of books; they are dynamic spaces where communities come together. They offer a safe, welcoming environment where people of all ages can gather, interact, and participate in a variety of educational and cultural activities. By providing free access to books, digital resources, and a range of programmes, libraries help bridge the gap between different socioeconomic groups, promoting equality and inclusiveness.

In neighbourhoods where resources may be limited, a local library becomes a crucial hub for learning and personal development. It serves as a venue for workshops, literacy programmes, and cultural events, fostering a sense of belonging and community pride. For children, libraries provide a space for after-school activities and summer reading programmes that keep them engaged and learning year-round. For adults, they offer opportunities for lifelong learning, skill development, and social interaction.

The Benefits of Reading

Reading is a fundamental skill that opens doors to a wealth of knowledge and opportunities. The benefits of reading extend far beyond academic achievement. It enhances cognitive development, improves concentration and focus, and fosters empathy by allowing readers to experience different perspectives and cultures. Regular reading habits are linked to enhanced language skills, better critical thinking, and a more profound understanding of the world.

In a world increasingly dominated by digital media, reading books can provide a much-needed respite from screens, helping reduce stress and improve mental health. For children, early exposure to reading is crucial for developing literacy skills that will serve as the foundation for their future education and career success. For adults, reading can be a form of continual education, keeping their minds sharp and engaged.

The Impact of the GiveBack to Algeria Initiative

The GiveBack to Algeria initiative's focus on creating a chain of libraries in every neighbourhood is a visionary step towards empowering communities and nurturing a culture of reading. By ensuring that everyone has access to a well-stocked library, the initiative addresses educational disparities and promotes intellectual growth across all age groups.

Each library established under this initiative will serve as a beacon of knowledge and a testament to the power of community-driven development. These libraries will not only provide access to books and educational materials but also create opportunities for individuals to come together, share ideas, and support one another. They will be spaces where young minds are inspired, where lifelong learning is encouraged, and where the rich cultural heritage of Algeria is celebrated and preserved.

In conclusion, establishing a chain of libraries in every neighbourhood as part of the GiveBack to Algeria initiative is a crucial investment in the nation's future. It recognises the invaluable role that libraries play in enhancing education, fostering community, and promoting the joy of reading. By supporting this initiative, we are taking a significant step towards building a more informed, connected, and empowered society.

Market Research and Planning:

Comprehensive market research will be conducted to identify neighbourhoods with the greatest need for libraries, understand the specific requirements of different communities, and assess the feasibility of each project. Strategic partnerships with educational institutions and cultural organisations will be established to enhance the range of programmes and services offered. Detailed planning will ensure that each library is designed to meet modern standards of accessibility, technology, and sustainability. Community engagement will be a key aspect of the planning process, ensuring that the libraries serve the needs and preferences of residents.

7. Swimming Pool in Each Neighbourhood (12.5% of Project Funding)
- o Total Allocation: €413,437,500
- o Estimated Number of Projects: 270 swimming pools
- o Average Cost per Project: €1,531,250

Project Description

GiveBack to Algeria: Building a Legacy of Swimming Excellence

In a remarkable move towards community enrichment and athletic excellence, the "GiveBack to Algeria" initiative has launched a chain of swimming pools in neighbourhoods across the country. This ambitious project aims not only to provide recreational facilities but also to cultivate a culture of swimming, leveraging Algeria's advantageous position along the Mediterranean coast to foster future champions and Olympians.

The Benefits of Swimming

Swimming is renowned for its myriad health benefits. It is a full-body workout that improves cardiovascular health, builds muscular strength, and enhances flexibility. Moreover, swimming is a low-impact exercise, making it accessible to people of all ages and physical conditions. Regular swimming sessions can improve mental health by reducing stress and anxiety, while also promoting social interaction and community bonding.

Harnessing Algeria's Coastal Advantage

Algeria boasts an extensive Mediterranean coastline stretching over 1,600 kilometres. This coastal advantage presents a unique opportunity to develop a strong swimming culture. The GiveBack to Algeria initiative is designed to tap into this potential, encouraging communities to embrace swimming as both a recreational and competitive activity. The availability of swimming pools in neighbourhoods makes it easier for residents to swim regularly, fostering a deeper connection with water sports.

Nurturing Future Champions

By providing accessible, high-quality swimming facilities, the initiative seeks to identify and nurture young talent who could represent Algeria in international competitions. The swimming pools are equipped with modern amenities and staffed by trained coaches who can provide professional training to aspiring swimmers. Early exposure to professional swimming training can significantly enhance young swimmers' skills and confidence, setting them on a path to become future champions.

Supporting International Competition

With the establishment of these swimming facilities, Algeria is poised to make a significant impact on the international swimming stage. The initiative aims to create a pipeline of well-trained athletes who can compete in events such as the Olympics, World Championships, and other international meets. By investing in the development of young swimmers, Algeria not only enhances its potential for sporting success but also promotes national pride and unity through sports.

A Community-Centric Approach

The GiveBack to Algeria initiative emphasises community involvement. The swimming pools serve as community hubs where people can come together, learn new skills, and support each other's growth. Special programmes for children, women, and older people ensure that everyone has the opportunity to benefit from swimming. Additionally, community events and swimming competitions foster a spirit of healthy competition and camaraderie.

The GiveBack to Algeria initiative is more than just a chain of swimming pools; it is a visionary project that aims to transform lives and elevate the country's status in the world of swimming. By leveraging Algeria's coastal advantage and focusing on the holistic benefits of swimming, the initiative is set to make a lasting impact on the health, well-being, and sporting success of Algerian communities. As the next generation of swimmers dives into these new pools, the dream of seeing Algerian athletes on the international podiums becomes ever more attainable.

Market Research and Planning:

Comprehensive market research will be conducted to identify optimal locations for the swimming pools, understand the needs and preferences of different communities, and assess the feasibility of each project. Detailed planning will ensure that the swimming pools meet modern safety, accessibility, and sustainability standards. Partnerships with local schools and sports organisations will be established to enhance the range of programmes and training offered. Community engagement will be a key aspect of the planning process, ensuring that the swimming pools serve the needs and preferences of residents.

8. Museum, Theatre, and Art Gallery in Each City (10% of Project Funding)

  o   Total Allocation: €320,625,000

  o   Estimated Number of Projects: fifty-four complexes (one in each major city)

  o   Average Cost per Project: €5,937,500

Project Description

The GiveBack to Algeria Initiative: Revitalising Theatre Across Cities

The "GiveBack to Algeria" initiative is a groundbreaking project that aims to rejuvenate Algeria's cultural landscape by establishing a chain of theatres across various cities. This initiative is not just about constructing buildings; it is about fostering a cultural renaissance that pays homage to Algeria's rich theatrical heritage while providing a platform for contemporary expression.

Why Theatre?

Theatre has always been a mirror to society, reflecting its values, struggles, and triumphs. In Algeria, theatre holds a special place in the hearts of the people, serving as a conduit for storytelling, cultural expression, and social commentary. By focusing on theatre, the GiveBack to Algeria initiative taps into this deep-seated cultural practice, aiming to revive and celebrate it. Theatre is not just an art form but a communal experience that brings people together, fostering dialogue and understanding.

The Importance of Theatre

Theatre is vital for several reasons:

4. Cultural Preservation: Theatre helps preserve Algeria's rich cultural narratives and traditions, passing them down to future generations.

5. Education: It serves as an educational tool, teaching history, social issues, and moral lessons in an engaging way.

6. Community Building: Theatre fosters a sense of community by bringing people together to share in a collective storytelling experience.

7. Economic Benefits: Theatres generate economic activity, providing jobs and stimulating local economies through tourism and related activities.

8. Artistic Expression: For artists, theatre offers a platform to express creativity, challenge norms, and inspire change.

Algerian Theatrical Heritage

Algeria has a storied history in theatre, with iconic institutions and figures that have shaped its trajectory. The Théâtre National Algérien (TNA), named after Mahieddine Bachtarzi, stands as a testament to the country's vibrant theatrical tradition. Bachtarzi, a luminary in Algerian theatre, dedicated his life to the performing arts, and his legacy continues to inspire.

Other notable figures include Kateb Yacine, whose play "Les Ancêtres redoublent de férocité" is a seminal work, and Abdelkader Alloula, known for his play "Le Médecin malgré lui," which adapts Molière's work to an Algerian context. These plays and artists have not only entertained but also provoked thought and encouraged discourse on critical social issues.

Multi-Use Spaces

The new theatres in the GiveBack to Algeria initiative are designed as multi-use spaces, versatile enough to host a variety of events:

o Performances: The primary use will be for theatrical performances, showcasing both traditional and contemporary works.

o Workshops: These spaces will host workshops and training sessions for aspiring actors, directors, and playwrights, nurturing the next generation of talent.

o Community Events: The theatres will serve as venues for community events, from school plays to public forums, ensuring they are integral parts of the community.

o   Exhibitions: Art exhibitions and cultural displays can be housed in these spaces, providing a venue for visual artists as well.

o   Film Screenings: Theatres can also be used for film screenings, broadening their cultural impact.

Benefits to the Community and Artists

The GiveBack to Algeria initiative brings numerous benefits to both the community and the artists:

14. Cultural Enrichment: Communities gain access to high-quality artistic experiences, enriching their lives and broadening their horizons.

15. Economic Growth: Theatres attract visitors, boosting local businesses and creating jobs.

16. Skill Development: Artists and community members can develop new skills through workshops and training programmes.

17. Social Cohesion: The communal nature of theatre fosters social cohesion, bringing people together to share experiences and engage in dialogue.

18. Artistic Platform: Artists gain a platform to showcase their work, reach broader audiences, and earn a livelihood through their craft.

The GiveBack to Algeria initiative is more than just a series of new theatres; it is a revival of a treasured cultural practice that holds immense importance in Algerian society. By creating spaces that honour the past and embrace the future, this initiative promises to enrich lives, foster community spirit, and invigorate Algeria's artistic landscape. Through theatre, the initiative seeks to weave a richer, more vibrant cultural tapestry for generations to come.

Market Research and Planning:

Comprehensive market research will be conducted to identify cities and locations with the highest demand for cultural venues, understand local community preferences, and analyse the competition. Detailed feasibility studies will assess the potential demand and profitability of each theatre. Partnerships with regional and international cultural organisations will be established to enhance the range of programmes and performances offered. Detailed business plans will outline operational strategies, marketing initiatives, and financial projections to ensure sustainable growth and community engagement.

9. Electric Bus for Transportation Between Neighbourhoods in the Same City (10% of Project Funding)
- o Total Allocation: €320,625,000
- o Estimated Number of Projects: twenty-seven bus networks
- o Average Cost per Project: €11,907,407

Project Description

GiveBack to Algeria: Modernising Urban Transport with Electric Buses

The "GiveBack to Algeria" initiative is committed to enhancing urban mobility and reducing environmental impact by introducing electric buses for inter-neighbourhood transport within the same city. This project aims to provide a sustainable, efficient, and accessible public transport system that reduces reliance on private vehicles and alleviates urban congestion.

Environmental Benefits

Electric buses produce zero emissions, significantly reducing air pollution from carbon dioxide, nitrogen oxides, and particulate matter. This transition to electric transport will improve air quality, contributing to a healthier urban environment and reducing the carbon footprint of Algeria's cities.

Efficiency and Reliability

Electric buses are known for their efficiency and reliability. They offer smooth, quiet rides with fewer mechanical issues than traditional diesel buses. The implementation of advanced route-planning and scheduling technologies will ensure buses operate efficiently, reducing waiting times and improving the overall public transport experience.

Economic Advantages

While the initial investment in electric buses and charging infrastructure is substantial, the long-term operational costs are lower. Electric buses have fewer moving parts, resulting in lower maintenance costs. Additionally, electricity as a fuel source is lower-cost and more stable than diesel, providing economic savings over time.

Enhancing Accessibility

The electric bus networks will be designed to enhance accessibility, with routes connecting key neighbourhoods, business districts, educational institutions, and healthcare facilities. This will provide residents with convenient, affordable transport options, reducing the need for private cars and promoting a more inclusive public transport system.

Supporting Local Manufacturing

The project will explore opportunities to collaborate with local manufacturers to produce and maintain electric buses. This will stimulate the local economy, create jobs, and promote the development of a domestic electric vehicle industry.

Community Engagement

Community engagement will be a key aspect of the project. Residents will be involved in the planning process to ensure that the bus routes and schedules meet their needs. Educational campaigns will raise awareness of the benefits of electric transport and encourage the use of public transport.

The introduction of electric buses under the GiveBack to Algeria initiative represents a significant step towards sustainable urban mobility. By providing efficient, reliable, and environmentally friendly public transport options, the project aims to reduce urban congestion, improve air quality, and enhance the quality of life for Algerian residents. This initiative aligns with global trends towards greener transportation and positions Algeria as a leader in sustainable urban development.

Market Research and Planning:

Comprehensive market research will be conducted to identify cities and routes with the highest demand for public transport, understand residents' travel patterns, and assess the feasibility of electric bus networks. Detailed planning will ensure that the bus networks meet modern standards of safety, accessibility, and sustainability. Partnerships with local and international transport experts will be established to leverage best practices and technologies. Community engagement will be a key aspect of the planning process, ensuring that the electric bus networks serve the needs and preferences of residents.

10. Car Park in Each City (10% of Project Funding)
    o   Total Allocation: €320,625,000
    o   Estimated Number of Projects: fifty-four car parks (one in each major city)
    o   Average Cost per Project: €5,937,500

Project Description

The GiveBack to Algeria Initiative: Transforming Urban Mobility with Car Parks

The "GiveBack to Algeria" initiative has introduced a transformative concept in urban mobility by establishing a chain of car parks across various city parts. This ambitious project aims to reduce reliance on cars in city centres, thereby reclaiming urban spaces for pedestrians and promoting a cleaner, healthier environment.

Modern cities are increasingly grappling with congestion and pollution, issues that not only impact the quality of life but also pose significant health risks. The overreliance on cars exacerbates these problems, with streets clogged by traffic and air quality deteriorating due to vehicle emissions. In response, the "GiveBack to Algeria" initiative has strategically located car parks on the periphery of city centres, encouraging residents and visitors to park and explore the city on foot or by public transport.

One of the core objectives of this initiative is to free the pavements and streets for pedestrians. In many cities, sidewalks are often obstructed by parked cars, leaving little space for people to walk comfortably. By relocating parking facilities to designated car parks, the initiative aims to create spacious, car-free zones where pedestrians can move freely and safely. This not only enhances the aesthetic appeal of urban areas but also fosters a more vibrant street life, with opportunities for outdoor cafes, markets, and public gatherings.

Reducing the number of cars in city centres also directly affects pollution levels. Fewer vehicles mean lower emissions of harmful pollutants such as carbon dioxide, nitrogen oxides, and particulate matter. This shift contributes to cleaner air and a healthier environment, benefiting both residents and the urban ecosystem. Moreover, lower traffic levels lead to quieter, more peaceful neighbourhoods, thereby improving the overall quality of urban living.

In addition to environmental benefits, the initiative promotes a more active lifestyle. Encouraging walking and public transport use helps combat the sedentary lifestyle associated with car dependency. With more walking spaces available, people are motivated to incorporate physical activity into their daily routines, thereby improving health outcomes.

The "GiveBack to Algeria" initiative is a forward-thinking approach to urban planning that addresses the multifaceted challenges of modern cities. By reducing car usage, freeing pavements for pedestrians, lowering pollution levels, and promoting walking, it paves the way for more liveable, sustainable, and vibrant urban environments. As cities across Algeria adopt this model, they set a precedent for others to follow, demonstrating how thoughtful, community-focused planning can transform urban landscapes.

Market Research and Planning:

Comprehensive market research will be conducted to identify optimal locations for the car parks, understand the parking needs and preferences of residents and visitors, and assess the feasibility of each project. Detailed planning will ensure that the car parks meet modern safety, accessibility, and sustainability standards. Partnerships with local and international urban planning experts will be established to leverage best practices and technologies. Community engagement will be a key aspect of the planning process, ensuring that the car parks serve the needs and preferences of residents.

Revenue and Profit Projections

Revenue Projections

The following are the projected revenues for each project type over the years, starting to generate revenue at the end of year 2, based on industry standards and expected market conditions.

1. **Chain of Supermarkets**
   - o   Annual Revenue per Supermarket: €10,000,000
      - o   Total Annual Revenue for 50 Supermarkets: €500,000,000
      - o   Total Revenue Over 5.5 Years: €2,750,000,000

2. **Chain of Hotels**
   - o   Annual Revenue per Hotel: €5,000,000
      - o   Total Annual Revenue for 20 Hotels: €100,000,000
      - o   Total Revenue Over 5.5 Years: €550,000,000

3. **Chain of Shops for Him and Her**
   - o   Annual Revenue per Shop: €1,000,000
   - o   Total Annual Revenue for one hundred Shops: €100,000,000
      - o   Total Revenue Over 5.5 Years: €550,000,000

4. **Apartment Buildings**
   - o   Annual Revenue per Building: €1,000,000
   - o   Total Annual Revenue for one hundred Buildings: €100,000,000
      - o   Total Revenue Over 5.5 Years: €550,000,000

5. Logistics, Storage, and Distribution Centres
      - o   Annual Revenue per Centre: €3,000,000
      - o   Total Annual Revenue for 30 Centres: €90,000,000
      - o   Total Revenue Over 5.5 Years: €495,000,000

6. Libraries

o   Annual Revenue per Library (through events, memberships): €50,000
   - o   Total Annual Revenue for 270 Libraries: €13,500,000
   - o   Total Revenue Over 5.5 Years: €74,250,000

7. Swimming Pools

o   Annual Revenue per Pool (through memberships, events): €50,000
   - o   Total Annual Revenue for 270 Pools: €13,500,000
   - o   Total Revenue Over 5.5 Years: €74,250,000

8. Museum, Theatre, and Art Gallery Complexes
   - o   Annual Revenue per Complex: €500,000
   - o   Total Annual Revenue for 54 Complexes: €27,000,000
   - o   Total Revenue Over 5.5 Years: €148,500,000

9. Electric Bus Networks

o   Annual Revenue per Network: €2,000,000
   - o   Total Annual Revenue for 27 Networks: €54,000,000
   - o   Total Revenue Over 5.5 Years: €297,000,000

10. Car Parks

o   Annual Revenue per Car Park: €500,000
   - o   Total Annual Revenue for 54 Car Parks: €27,000,000
   - o   Total Revenue Over 5.5 Years: €148,500,000

Total Revenue Over 5.5 Years

- • Total Revenue for All Projects: €5,637,500,000

(Note: These projections assume that revenue generation will commence at the end of year 2, aligning with industry standards and market expectations.)

Profit Projections

The following are detailed profit projections for each project type over the years, assuming a 20% profit margin.

1. **Chain of Supermarkets**
   - o   Annual Revenue per Supermarket: €10,000,000
     - o   Total Annual Revenue for 50 Supermarkets: €500,000,000
     - o   Total Revenue Over 5.5 Years: €2,750,000,000
     - o   Profit Margin: 20%
     - o   Total Profit Over 5.5 Years: €550,000,000

2. **Chain of Hotels**
   - o   Annual Revenue per Hotel: €5,000,000
     - o   Total Annual Revenue for 20 Hotels: €100,000,000
     - o   Total Revenue Over 5.5 Years: €550,000,000
     - o   Profit Margin: 20%
     - o   Total Profit Over 5.5 Years: €110,000,000

3. **Chain of Shops for Him and Her**
   - o   Annual Revenue per Shop: €1,000,000
     - o   Total Annual Revenue for one hundred Shops: €100,000,000
     - o   Total Revenue Over 5.5 Years: €550,000,000
     - o   Profit Margin: 20%
     - o   Total Profit Over 5.5 Years: €110,000,000

4. **Apartment Buildings**
   - o   Annual Revenue per Building: €1,000,000
     - o   Total Annual Revenue for one hundred Buildings: €100,000,000
     - o   Total Revenue Over 5.5 Years: €550,000,000
     - o   Profit Margin: 20%
     - o   Total Profit Over 5.5 Years: €110,000,000

5. Logistics, Storage, and Distribution Centres
     - o   Annual Revenue per Centre: €3,000,000
     - o   Total Annual Revenue for 30 Centres: €90,000,000
     - o   Total Revenue Over 5.5 Years: €495,000,000
     - o   Profit Margin: 20%
     - o   Total Profit Over 5.5 Years: €99,000,000

6. **Libraries**
   - o   Annual Revenue per Library (through events, memberships): €50,000
     - o   Total Annual Revenue for 270 Libraries: €13,500,000

- o   Total Revenue Over 5.5 Years: €74,250,000
- o   Profit Margin: 20%
- o   Total Profit Over 5.5 Years: €14,850,000

7. Swimming Pools

- o   Annual Revenue per Pool (through memberships, events): €50,000
  - o   Total Annual Revenue for 270 Pools: €13,500,000
  - o   Total Revenue Over 5.5 Years: €74,250,000
  - o   Profit Margin: 20%
  - o   Total Profit Over 5.5 Years: €14,850,000

8. Museum, Theatre, and Art Gallery Complexes
- o   Annual Revenue per Complex: €500,000
- o   Total Annual Revenue for 54 Complexes: €27,000,000
- o   Total Revenue Over 5.5 Years: €148,500,000
- o   Profit Margin: 20%
- o   Total Profit Over 5.5 Years: €29,700,000

9. Electric Bus Networks

- o   Annual Revenue per Network: €2,000,000
- o   Total Annual Revenue for 27 Networks: €54,000,000
- o   Total Revenue Over 5.5 Years: €297,000,000
- o   Profit Margin: 20%
- o   Total Profit Over 5.5 Years: €59,400,000

10. Car Parks

- o   Annual Revenue per Car Park: €500,000
- o   Total Annual Revenue for 54 Car Parks: €27,000,000
- o   Total Revenue Over 5.5 Years: €148,500,000
- o   Profit Margin: 20%
- o   Total Profit Over 5.5 Years: €29,700,000

Total Profit Over 5.5 Years

- • Total Profit for All Projects: €1,128,300,000

(Note: These projections assume that revenue generation will commence at the end of year 2, aligning with industry standards and market expectations.)

Utilisation of Revenues and Profits

The revenues generated from these projects will be strategically reinvested into future ventures and the expansion of existing initiatives. This reinvestment strategy ensures the sustainability and growth of our projects, enabling us to innovate and meet the evolving needs of our community continuously.

All profits from the GiveBack to Algeria initiative are dedicated to funding new ventures, ensuring the initiative not only sustains itself but also expands its reach, thereby amplifying its impact on the Algerian population. By channelling profits into new and existing projects, we can address more areas of need and support a broader spectrum of beneficiaries.

A key focus of our reinvestment strategy is creating job opportunities. By funding new projects and expanding current ones, we generate a substantial number of jobs, directly benefiting the Algerian workforce. These employment opportunities span sectors such as education, healthcare, infrastructure, and technology, offering diverse career paths and contributing to the country's overall economic development. Our goal is to reduce unemployment rates and ensure that every Algerian can secure stable, meaningful employment.

Significantly, our reinvestment strategy centres on the people of Algeria. Profits are utilised to enhance the community's overall welfare, including funding educational programmes, healthcare improvements, and infrastructure projects. Additionally, we invest in cultural and sports competitions through sponsorships, fostering national pride and community spirit while promoting healthy lifestyles and cultural enrichment.

No shareholders are profiting from these revenues. Instead, every dinar earned is reinvested in the community. Our goal is to foster an environment where all Algerians can thrive and benefit from the collective success of our initiatives. This includes supporting cultural events that celebrate Algeria's rich heritage and sports programmes that encourage youth engagement and physical fitness.

Through this comprehensive reinvestment model, we are committed to driving long-term, sustainable development in Algeria, ensuring that future generations benefit from our projects. By focusing on people, new projects, community sponsorships, and job creation, we aim to create a robust, inclusive, and dynamic future for all Algerians.

Key Considerations for the "GiveBack to Algeria" Initiative

The "GiveBack to Algeria" initiative is an ambitious, comprehensive plan to transform various aspects of Algerian society through sustainable development projects. To ensure the initiative's success and long-term impact, several key considerations must be addressed. These considerations encompass financial planning, project management, community engagement, sustainability, regulatory compliance, and risk management, all tailored to Algeria's unique context.

1. Financial Planning and Budget Allocation

Detailed Budgeting

A meticulous budgeting process is essential to allocate resources effectively across different projects. Each project's funding allocation should be based on detailed cost estimates, including initial setup costs, operational expenses, and maintenance. Regular financial reviews and audits should be conducted to ensure that funds are being used efficiently and transparently. Given Algeria's economic conditions, careful attention must be paid to cost management and resource allocation.

Revenue Generation

While the initiative aims to foster development, it is crucial to ensure that the projects generate sufficient revenue to be self-sustaining. Detailed revenue projections should be prepared for each project, factoring in local market demand, pricing strategies, and competition. Profits generated from these projects will be reinvested in future ventures and expansions, ensuring continuous growth and development that directly benefits Algerians.

Contingency Planning

A portion of the budget should be allocated for contingencies to address unforeseen expenses or project delays. This ensures that projects can proceed without significant financial disruptions, especially considering the potential volatility of the local economy.

2. Project Management

Comprehensive Planning

Each project within the initiative requires a detailed project plan outlining the objectives, timelines, milestones, and deliverables. This plan should also include a resource-allocation strategy to ensure that human, financial, and material resources are distributed appropriately.

Skilled Project Teams

Forming competent project teams with the necessary skills and experience is crucial for the successful implementation of each project. This includes hiring experienced project managers, engineers, architects, financial analysts, and community engagement specialists, ideally from within Algeria, to maximise local expertise and employment.

Monitoring and Evaluation

Establishing robust monitoring and evaluation mechanisms is vital to tracking each project's progress. Key performance indicators (KPIs) should be defined to measure the success and impact of the projects. Regular progress reports and evaluations will help identify areas for improvement and ensure that the projects remain on track.

3. Community Engagement

Stakeholder Involvement

Engaging local communities and stakeholders is critical to the initiative's success. This includes involving community leaders, local businesses, residents, and government officials in the planning and implementation processes. Their input and support are vital for ensuring that the projects meet the needs and expectations of the communities they serve.

Transparent Communication

Maintaining transparent and open communication with all stakeholders is essential. Regular updates on project progress, challenges, and achievements should be shared through various communication channels, including community meetings, newsletters, and social media. In Algeria, leveraging traditional communication methods alongside digital platforms can help reach a wider audience.

Cultural Sensitivity

Respecting and incorporating local cultural values and practices into the projects is essential for community acceptance and support. This involves understanding the cultural context of each region and ensuring that the projects align with local traditions and preferences. For instance, designing projects that reflect Algerian architectural styles and cultural heritage can enhance local pride and engagement.

4. Sustainability

Environmental Considerations

All projects should be designed and implemented with a focus on sustainability. This includes using eco-friendly materials, adopting energy-efficient technologies, and implementing waste reduction practices. Environmental impact assessments should be conducted to ensure that projects do not harm local ecosystems, particularly in ecologically sensitive areas such as the Sahara Desert and the Mediterranean coast.

Social Sustainability

Ensuring that the projects contribute to the long-term well-being of the communities is crucial. This involves providing training and employment opportunities to residents, supporting local businesses, and creating spaces that promote social cohesion and community development.

Economic Sustainability

The projects should be economically sustainable, generating sufficient revenue to cover their operational costs and contribute to future development. This involves careful market research, competitive pricing strategies, and continuous innovation to meet market demands.

5. Regulatory Compliance

Adhering to Local Laws

All projects must comply with local, regional, and national regulations. This includes obtaining the necessary permits and approvals, adhering to building codes and safety standards, and ensuring that all legal requirements are met.

International Standards

Where applicable, projects should also align with international standards and best practices. This enhances the quality and credibility of the projects and ensures that they meet global benchmarks for sustainability, safety, and efficiency.

6. Risk Management

Identifying Risks

A comprehensive risk assessment should be conducted for each project to identify potential risks and challenges. These can include financial, operational, environmental, and social risks.

Mitigation Strategies

Developing and implementing effective risk mitigation strategies is essential to minimise the impact of potential risks. This involves creating contingency plans, diversifying funding sources, ensuring regulatory compliance, and maintaining open communication with stakeholders.

Continuous Monitoring

Risk management is an ongoing process that requires continuous monitoring and adjustment. Regular risk assessments and reviews should be conducted to identify new risks and evaluate the effectiveness of mitigation strategies.

The "GiveBack to Algeria" initiative is a visionary plan to transform Algeria's socio-economic landscape. By addressing these key considerations, the initiative can ensure that its projects are effectively planned, managed, and executed. This comprehensive approach will maximise the initiative's impact, fostering sustainable development and improving the quality of life for Algerian communities. With careful planning, community engagement, and a commitment to sustainability, the "GiveBack to Algeria" initiative can achieve its mission of honouring Algeria's legacy and building a brighter future for all.

Project Breakdown Structure (PBS) for the "GiveBack to Algeria" Initiative

The Project Breakdown Structure (PBS) is a hierarchical representation of the deliverables and components of the "GiveBack to Algeria" initiative. It breaks down the overall initiative into manageable sections, ensuring each aspect is comprehensively planned and executed.

Level 0: "GiveBack to Algeria" Initiative

1. Historical Overview and Context
    o Algerian Independence History
    o Nationalist Movements
    o Cultural and Social Context
2. Financial Planning and Budget Allocation
    o Detailed Budgeting
    o **Revenue Generation**
    o **Contingency Planning**
3. Project Management
    o **Comprehensive Planning**
    o **Skilled Project Teams**
    o **Monitoring and Evaluation**
4. **Community Engagement**
    o **Stakeholder Involvement**
    o Transparent Communication

- o Cultural Sensitivity
5. Sustainability
   - o Environmental Considerations
   - o Social Sustainability
   - o Economic Sustainability
6. Regulatory Compliance
   - o Adhering to Local Laws
   - o International Standards
7. Risk Management
   - o Identifying Risks
   - o Mitigation Strategies
   - o Continuous Monitoring

Level 1: Major Projects

1. Chain of Supermarkets
   - o **Market Research and Planning**
   - o **Site Selection**
   - o Construction
   - o Stock Management Systems
   - o **Operations and Management**
   - o **Community Engagement**

2. Chain of Hotels
   - o **Market Research and Planning**
   - o **Site Selection**
   - o Construction
   - o Interior Design
   - o **Operations and Management**
   - o **Community Engagement**

3. Chain of Shops for Him and Her
   - o **Market Research and Planning**
   - o **Site Selection**
   - o Construction
   - o Product Sourcing
   - o **Operations and Management**
   - o **Community Engagement**

4. Apartment Buildings Across Algeria
   o **Market Research and Planning**
   o **Site Selection**
   o Construction
   o Community Facilities (After School Clubs)
   o **Operations and Management**
   o **Community Engagement**

5. Logistics, Storage, and Distribution Centres
   o **Market Research and Planning**
   o **Site Selection**
   o Construction
   o Technology Implementation
   o **Operations and Management**
   o **Community Engagement**

6. Library in Each Neighbourhood
   o **Market Research and Planning**
   o **Site Selection**
   o Construction
   o Stocking and Resource Management
   o **Operations and Management**
   o **Community Engagement**

7. Swimming Pool in Each Neighbourhood
   o **Market Research and Planning**
   o **Site Selection**
   o Construction
   o **Facilities Management**
   o **Operations and Management**
   o **Community Engagement**

8. Museum, Theatre, and Art Gallery in Each City
   o **Market Research and Planning**
   o **Site Selection**
   o Construction
   o Exhibits and Programmes Planning
   o **Operations and Management**
   o **Community Engagement**

9. Electric Bus Networks for Transportation Between Neighbourhoods in the Same City

- o **Market Research and Planning**
- o Route Planning
- o Bus Acquisition and Infrastructure
- o **Operations and Management**
- o **Community Engagement**

10. Car Park in Each City
- o **Market Research and Planning**
- o **Site Selection**
- o Construction
- o Technology Implementation (e.g., ticketing systems)
- o **Operations and Management**
- o **Community Engagement**

Level 2: Sub-Projects/Components within Each Major Project

1. Chain of Supermarkets

- o Site Planning and Permits
  - **Feasibility Studies**
  - **Permitting and Approvals**
- o **Design and Construction**
  - **Architectural Design**
  - **Construction Management**
- o Supply Chain Set-up
  - Vendor Contracts
  - Logistics Planning
- o **Technology Integration**
  - Stock Management Systems
  - POS Systems
- o **Marketing and Launch**
  - **Branding and Promotion**
  - Community Outreach

2. Chain of Hotels

- o Site Planning and Permits
  - **Feasibility Studies**
  - **Permitting and Approvals**
- o **Design and Construction**
  - **Architectural Design**

- Interior Design
- **Construction Management**
  - Service Development
    - Hospitality Training
    - Service Protocols
  - **Technology Integration**
    - Reservation Systems
    - Guest Management Systems
  - **Marketing and Launch**
    - **Branding and Promotion**
    - Community Outreach

3. **Chain of Shops for Him and Her**
  - Site Planning and Permits
    - **Feasibility Studies**
    - **Permitting and Approvals**
  - **Design and Construction**
    - **Architectural Design**
    - Interior Layout
    - **Construction Management**
  - Inventory Management
    - Product Sourcing
    - Stock Management
  - **Technology Integration**
    - POS Systems
    - Inventory Tracking Systems
  - **Marketing and Launch**
    - **Branding and Promotion**
    - Community Outreach

4. Apartment Buildings Across Algeria
  - Site Planning and Permits
    - **Feasibility Studies**
    - **Permitting and Approvals**
  - **Design and Construction**
    - **Architectural Design**
    - **Construction Management**
  - **Facilities Management**
    - After School Clubs Set-up

- Maintenance Planning
        - o **Community Engagement**
            - Resident Programmes
            - Community Events

5. Logistics, Storage, and Distribution Centres
    - o Site Planning and Permits
        - **Feasibility Studies**
        - **Permitting and Approvals**
    - o **Design and Construction**
        - **Architectural Design**
        - **Construction Management**
    - o **Technology Integration**
        - Inventory Systems
        - Logistics Management Systems
    - o Operations Set-up
        - Staffing and Training
        - Security Systems

6. Library in Each Neighbourhood
    - o Site Planning and Permits
        - **Feasibility Studies**
        - **Permitting and Approvals**
    - o **Design and Construction**
        - **Architectural Design**
        - **Construction Management**
    - o Resource Management
        - Book and Digital Media Acquisition
        - Cataloguing Systems
    - o Programmes Development
        - Community Workshops
        - Educational Programmes

7. Swimming Pool in Each Neighbourhood
    - o Site Planning and Permits
        - **Feasibility Studies**
        - **Permitting and Approvals**
    - o **Design and Construction**
        - **Architectural Design**
        - **Construction Management**

- o **Facilities Management**
  - Maintenance Planning
  - Lifeguard and Staff Training
- o Community Programmes
  - Swimming Lessons
  - Recreational Events

8. Museum, Theatre, and Art Gallery in Each City
   - o Site Planning and Permits
     - **Feasibility Studies**
     - **Permitting and Approvals**
   - o **Design and Construction**
     - **Architectural Design**
     - **Construction Management**
   - o Exhibit Planning
     - Acquisition of Artefacts
     - Programme Scheduling
   - o **Community Engagement**
     - Cultural Events
     - Educational Workshops

9. Electric Bus Networks for Transportation Between Neighbourhoods in the Same City
   - o Route Planning and Permits
     - **Feasibility Studies**
     - **Permitting and Approvals**
   - o Fleet Acquisition
     - Bus Procurement
     - Infrastructure Set-up (Charging Stations)
   - o Operations Set-up
     - Route Scheduling
     - Driver Training
   - o Community Outreach
     - Awareness Campaigns
     - Ridership Programmes

10. Car Park in Each City
    - o Site Planning and Permits
      - **Feasibility Studies**
      - **Permitting and Approvals**

69

   o **Design and Construction**
     ▪ **Architectural Design**
     ▪ **Construction Management**
   o **Technology Integration**
     ▪ Ticketing Systems
     ▪ Security Systems
   o Operations Set-up
     ▪ Staffing and Training
     ▪ Maintenance Planning

The Project Breakdown Structure (PBS) for the "GiveBack to Algeria" initiative provides a detailed hierarchical view of all components required for its successful implementation. Each major project and its sub-projects are broken down into specific tasks, ensuring thorough planning, efficient resource allocation, and effective management. This structure will serve as a foundational guide for executing the initiative, achieving its goals, and maximising its impact on Algerian society.

Additional Resources for GiveBack to Algeria Initiative

To ensure the success and sustainability of the GiveBack to Algeria initiative, it is crucial to consider various additional resources, including human resources, technology, partnerships, community engagement, funding, and robust monitoring and evaluation systems.

1. Human Resources

Key Personnel:

- Project Managers: Oversee planning, execution, and completion of project components.
- Financial Analysts: Manage budgeting, financial planning, and reporting.
- Marketing and Communications Specialists: Develop and implement marketing strategies and manage public relations.
- Community Engagement Coordinators: Foster relationships with local communities and stakeholders.

- Operational Staff: Handle day-to-day operations for each project component (e.g., supermarket managers, hotel staff, library administrators).

Recruitment and Training:

- Recruitment Strategies: Develop robust strategies to attract qualified personnel.
- Training Programmes: Implement comprehensive training programmes to ensure staff are well-prepared and knowledgeable about their roles.

2. Technology

Infrastructure:

- IT Systems: Implement robust IT systems to manage operations, inventory, and customer relations.
- Online Platforms: Develop websites and mobile applications for project components like supermarkets, hotels, and libraries.

Tools and Software:

- Project Management Software: Utilise tools like Microsoft Project, Asana, or Trello to manage project timelines and tasks.
- Financial Management Software: Implement software like QuickBooks or SAP for financial tracking and reporting.
- Customer Relationship Management (CRM) Systems: Use CRM systems to manage customer interactions and data.

3. Partnerships

Strategic Partnerships:

- Government Partnerships: Collaborate with local and national governments for support and regulatory compliance.
- Corporate Partnerships: Partner with corporations for sponsorships, funding, and resources.

- Nonprofit Organisations: Work with nonprofits to leverage their expertise and resources in specific areas (e.g., education, healthcare).

Collaborative Initiatives:

- Public-Private Partnerships: Engage in public-private partnerships to share resources and expertise.
- Academic Partnerships: Collaborate with universities and research institutions for knowledge exchange and research opportunities.

4. Community Engagement

Stakeholder Engagement:

- Community Meetings: Hold regular meetings with community members to gather feedback and keep them informed about project progress.
- Surveys and Feedback: Conduct surveys to understand community needs and preferences.
- Volunteer Programmes: Encourage community members to volunteer and participate in project activities.

Awareness and Outreach:

- Marketing Campaigns: Develop marketing campaigns to raise awareness about the initiative and its benefits.
- Social Media Engagement: Use social media platforms to engage with the community and share updates.
- Events and Workshops: Organise events and workshops to educate the community about various project components and their impact.

5. Funding and Grants

Funding Sources:

- Crowdfunding Campaigns: Launch crowdfunding campaigns to raise funds from the global community.

- Grants: Apply for grants from government agencies, foundations, and international organisations.
- Corporate Sponsorships: Seek sponsorships from corporations interested in corporate social responsibility (CSR) initiatives.

Financial Planning:

- Budget Allocation: Ensure proper allocation of funds to each project component based on priority and need.
- Financial Monitoring: Implement robust financial monitoring systems to track expenditures and ensure accountability.

6. Monitoring and Evaluation

Key Performance Indicators (KPIs):

- Project Milestones: Set clear milestones for each project component to track progress.
- Financial Metrics: Monitor financial performance through metrics like revenue, profit margins, and return on investment (ROI).
- Impact Assessment: Evaluate the social and economic impact of the projects on the community.

Evaluation Methods:

- Regular Reporting: Prepare regular reports to track progress and financial performance.
- Third-Party Audits: Conduct third-party audits to ensure transparency and accountability.
- Community Feedback: Gather feedback from the community to assess the effectiveness and impact of the projects.

By leveraging these additional resources, the GiveBack to Algeria initiative can achieve its goals and create a lasting positive impact in Algeria. This comprehensive framework supports successful implementation and sustainability, ensuring that the initiative benefits the communities it aims to serve.

GiveBack to Algeria Initiative: Organisational Structure

1. Board of Directors

Roles and Responsibilities:

- Establish overall strategies and policies for the GiveBack to Algeria initiative.
- Monitor overall performance and ensure goals are met.
- Oversee financial operations to ensure transparency and accountability.

Members:

- Chairperson: Leads meetings and directs strategic decisions.
- Vice Chairperson: Supports the chairperson and acts in their absence.
- Board Members: Comprising influential figures from the Algerian diaspora, development experts, and local leaders in Algeria.

2. Executive Team

Roles and Responsibilities:

- Manage day-to-day operations and implement strategies set by the Board.
- Oversee fundraising and project implementation.
- Ensure continuous communication with donors and partners.

Members:

- Chief Executive Officer (CEO): Responsible for overall leadership and managing the executive team.
- Chief Financial Officer (CFO): Manages financial operations and financial reporting.
- Chief Operating Officer (COO): Oversees project implementation and daily operations.

- Chief Marketing and Communications Officer (CMO): Manages marketing campaigns and communications with donors and partners.
- Chief Human Resources Officer (CHRO): Manages team development and human resources.

3. Advisory Board

Roles and Responsibilities:

- Provide advice and guidance to the Board and Executive Team.
- Offer specialised expertise in areas such as education, healthcare, infrastructure, and entrepreneurship.
- Assist in evaluating project impact and ensuring quality.

Members:

- Education Expert: Provides advice on educational projects.
- Healthcare Expert: Provides advice on healthcare projects.
- Infrastructure Expert: Provides advice on infrastructure projects.
- Entrepreneurship Expert: Provides advice on entrepreneurship and small business support projects.

4. Project Teams

Roles and Responsibilities:

- Implement designated projects and ensure goal achievement.
- Communicate with local stakeholders and partners to ensure effective collaboration.
- Provide regular reports on project progress and challenges.

Members:

- Project Manager: Leads each project and ensures timeline and budget adherence.
- Engineers and Specialists: Work on technical and engineering aspects of projects.

- Site Managers: Oversee operations at project sites and ensure quality and safety.

5. Administrative Teams

Roles and Responsibilities:

- Support daily operations and ensure administrative efficiency.
- Manage financial and human resources.
- Provide technical and administrative support to project teams.

Members:

- Finance Staff: Manage accounts, budgets, and financial reporting.
- Human Resources Staff: Handle recruitment, training, and staff development.
- Technical Support Staff: Provide IT and technical support for information systems and communications.

6. Volunteer and Community Engagement Teams

Roles and Responsibilities:

- Enhance community involvement and support projects through volunteer efforts.
- Organise community events and participate in awareness campaigns.
- Gather feedback from local communities to ensure needs are met.

Members:

- Volunteer Coordinator: Manages volunteer teams and organises volunteer activities.
- Local Volunteers: Participate in project implementation and community activities.
- Community Coordinators: Gather feedback and communicate with local communities.

Recruitment Plan

Join the GiveBack to Algeria Initiative

This section outlines the key roles needed during the preparation and early delivery phases. GBTA is currently in the preparation phase; many early roles may be voluntary and unpaid until formal registration and launch. Any paid roles will be formalised through Al Amana Development under proper contracts and governance.

Available Positions:

1. Project Managers

- Location: Algeria
- **Responsibilities:**
    o   Oversee the planning, implementation, and tracking of specific short-term projects.
    o   Ensure projects are completed on time, within budget, and meet high-quality standards.
    o   Coordinate with local stakeholders and partners.
- **Qualifications:**
    o   Proven experience in project management.
    o   Strong leadership and organisational skills.
    o   Excellent communication and interpersonal abilities.

2. Marketing and Communications Officers

- Location: Remote/Algeria
- **Responsibilities:**
    o   Develop and implement marketing strategies to promote the initiative.
    o   Manage social media accounts and create engaging content.
    o   Coordinate with media outlets and manage public relations.
- **Qualifications:**
    o   Experience in marketing, communications, or related fields.
    o   Proficiency in social media management and content creation.

o   Strong writing and communication skills.

3. Fundraising Coordinators

- Location: Remote/Algeria
- **Responsibilities:**
    o   Develop and execute fundraising campaigns.
    o   Build and maintain relationships with donors and sponsors.
    o   Organise fundraising events and activities.
- **Qualifications:**
    o   Experience in fundraising or sales.
    o   Excellent networking and relationship-building skills.
    o   Ability to work independently and as part of a team.

4. Legal Advisors

- Location: Remote/Algeria
- **Responsibilities:**
    o   Provide legal advice and support on various aspects of the initiative.
    o   Ensure compliance with local and international laws and regulations.
    o   Draft, review, and negotiate contracts and agreements.
- **Qualifications:**
    o   Degree in law with relevant experience.
    o   Strong understanding of Algerian and international legal systems.
    o   Excellent analytical and critical thinking skills.

5. Community Engagement Officers

- Location: Algeria
- **Responsibilities:**
    o   Engage with local communities to understand their needs and priorities.
    o   Facilitate community meetings and feedback sessions.
    o   Coordinate community-based projects and activities.

- **Qualifications:**
    - o Experience in community development or social work.
    - o Strong interpersonal and communication skills.
    - o Ability to work collaboratively with diverse groups.

How to Apply

If you are interested in contributing, please email your CV and a short note explaining your interest and availability to info@givebacktoalgeria.com. Please indicate whether you can support the preparation phase as a volunteer, or whether you are expressing interest in future employment opportunities after the formal launch.

- Recruitment timetable: to be published upon formal registration and launch.

GiveBack to Algeria – Building Tomorrow, Today.

How to Proceed with All the Projects of the GiveBack to Algeria Initiative

The strategy for implementing the projects of the GiveBack to Algeria initiative involves a phased approach to ensure comprehensive and sustainable development across Algeria. The plan is as follows:

1. Initial Phase: Set up One of Each Project in Each Wilaya
    - o Objective: Establish a presence in each of the 69 wilayas (provinces) of Algeria by setting up one of each project.
    - o Outcome: This will create a solid foundation and demonstrate the initiative's impact across the entire country.
2. Second Phase: Expand to Each Daira
    - o Objective: Once a presence is established in each wilaya, the next step is to implement one of each project in each daira (district) within the wilayas.
    - o Outcome: This phase will ensure that the benefits of the initiative reach more minor administrative divisions, further decentralising development efforts.
3. Final Phase: Presence in Each Commune

o   Objective: The final phase involves extending the projects to every commune (municipality) within the dairas.

o   Outcome: By reaching the commune level, the initiative will ensure that even the most local communities benefit from the projects, promoting equitable development across Algeria.

Administrative System in Algeria

- Wilayas (Provinces): Algeria is divided into 69 wilayas, each governed by a wali (governor) appointed by the President of Algeria. Wilayas serve as the primary administrative divisions.
- Daïras (Districts): Each wilaya is further divided into daïras (districts), which group several communes and support the coordination of local administration.
- Communes (Municipalities): The most minor administrative units are communes (municipalities). Algeria has 1,541 communes nationwide, each governed by an elected municipal council responsible for local administration and services.

Year 1: Foundation & Planning for GiveBack to Algeria Initiative

Overview

The first year is crucial for laying a solid foundation for the "GiveBack to Algeria" initiative. This year should focus on establishing the necessary infrastructure, building partnerships, and creating detailed plans for the successful implementation of the project components.

Detailed Plan for Year 1

1. Establish Organisational Structure

Key Actions:

- Form a Core Team: Recruit key personnel, including project managers, financial analysts, marketing specialists, community engagement coordinators, and operational staff.

- Define Roles and Responsibilities: Clearly outline the roles and responsibilities of each team member to ensure efficient project management.
- Create Advisory Board: Establish an advisory board comprising experts in various fields to provide strategic guidance and oversight.

2. Secure Initial Funding

Key Actions:

- Fundraising Campaign: Launch a comprehensive fundraising campaign targeting the Algerian diaspora, including crowdfunding and direct donation appeals.
- Apply for Grants: Identify and apply for grants from international organisations, foundations, and government programmes that support development initiatives.
- Corporate Sponsorships: Seek sponsorships from multinational corporations and local businesses interested in corporate social responsibility (CSR) initiatives.

3. Develop Detailed Project Plans

Key Actions:

- Project Planning: Develop detailed project plans for each component, including timelines, budgets, resource requirements, and risk management strategies.
- Feasibility Studies: Conduct feasibility studies for key projects to assess potential challenges and opportunities.
- Cost Estimation: Finalise cost estimates for construction, operational, and administrative expenses.

4. Build Strategic Partnerships

Key Actions:

- Government Collaboration: Engage with local and national government authorities to gain support, streamline regulatory processes, and access additional resources.
- NGO Partnerships: Form partnerships with NGOs and other charitable organisations to leverage their expertise and resources.
- Community Engagement: Establish relationships with local communities to ensure their involvement and support for the initiative.

5. Establish Operational Infrastructure

Key Actions:

- Office Set-up: Set up the head office and regional offices as needed to coordinate project activities.
- Technology Implementation: Implement essential technology infrastructure, including IT systems, fiscal management software, and Customer Relationship Management (CRM) systems.
- Online Presence: Develop a user-friendly website and social media platforms for information dissemination, donor engagement, and online donations.

6. Launch Initial Projects

Key Actions:

- Pilot Projects: Select a few key projects to launch as pilots to assess processes, gather data, and make necessary adjustments.
- Project Execution: Begin construction and implementation of the selected pilot projects, ensuring adherence to timelines and budgets.
- Monitoring and Evaluation: Implement monitoring and evaluation mechanisms to track progress, identify issues, and measure impact.

7. Engage and Retain Donors

Key Actions:

- Communication Strategy: Develop and implement a comprehensive communication strategy to keep donors informed and engaged.
- Regular Updates: Provide regular updates on project progress, financial status, and impact through newsletters, social media, and personalised messages.
- Recognition Programmes: Implement donor recognition programmes to acknowledge and reward loyal contributors.

8. Implement Financial Management Practices

Key Actions:

- Budgeting: Create detailed budgets for each project component and establish processes for regular financial reviews.
- Financial Monitoring: Use fiscal management software to track income, expenses, and cash flow in real-time.
- Audits: Conduct regular financial audits to ensure transparency, accountability, and compliance with regulatory requirements.

9. Develop Risk Management Plans

Key Actions:

- Risk Identification: Identify potential risks for each project component, including financial, operational, and regulatory risks.
- Mitigation Strategies: Develop and implement strategies to mitigate identified risks.
- Contingency Planning: Create contingency plans to address unexpected challenges and ensure continuity of operations.

10. Prepare for Year 2 Expansion

Key Actions:

- Review and Reflect: At the end of Year 1, conduct a thorough review of all activities, achievements, and challenges.

- Adjust Plans: Adjust project plans and strategies based on the learnings from Year 1.
- Set Goals for Year 2: Set clear goals and objectives for Year 2, focusing on scaling up successful projects and launching new ones.

Summary Timeline for Year 1

Quarter	Key Activities
Q1	Form core team, establish advisory board, secure initial funding.
Q2	Develop detailed project plans and build strategic partnerships.
Q3	Set up operational infrastructure, launch pilot projects.
Q4	Engage donors, implement financial practices, and prepare for Year 2

Year 1 is critical for establishing a solid foundation for the "GiveBack to Algeria" initiative. By focusing on building the organisational structure, securing funding, developing detailed plans, and launching initial projects, the initiative can set the stage for sustainable growth and success in the coming years.

Years 2-3: Building the Infrastructure for GiveBack to Algeria Initiative

Following the foundational work done in Year 1, Years 2 and 3 will focus on scaling up the initiative, building the necessary infrastructure, and expanding project implementations. Here is a detailed plan for Years 2 and 3:

Year 2: Scaling Up

1. Expand Project Implementations

Key Actions:

- Supermarket Chain: Start construction and set up for an additional twenty-five supermarkets.
- Hotel Chain: Begin construction for ten more hotels.
- Retail Shops: Launch fifty more retail shops for him and her.
- Apartment Buildings: Commence building twenty-five additional apartment buildings.

- Logistics Centres: Set up five more logistics, storage, and distribution centres.
- Libraries: Establish one hundred more libraries across various neighbourhoods.
- Swimming Pools: Construct one hundred additional swimming pools.
- Cultural Infrastructure: Start developing twenty more cultural infrastructure projects (museums, theatres, art galleries).
- Electric Bus Transportation: Implement five more bus routes.
- Car Parks: Develop twenty-five more car parks.

2. Strengthen Operational Capacity

Key Actions:

- Recruitment and Training: Hire and train staff for the new project components being launched.
- Technology Upgrades: Enhance IT systems, online platforms, and project management tools to support the expanded operations.
- Operational Efficiency: Implement best practices and process improvements to optimise operations across all projects.

3. Enhance Donor Engagement

Key Actions:

- Personalised Communication: Increase personalised communication with donors to keep them engaged and informed.
- Impact Stories: Share detailed impact stories and case studies demonstrating how donations are making a difference.
- Events and Campaigns: Organise donor appreciation events and fundraising campaigns to boost engagement and donations.

4. Secure Additional Funding

Key Actions:

- Grant Applications: Continue applying for grants to secure additional funding for expanded projects.
- Corporate Sponsorships: Seek new corporate sponsorships and renew existing ones.
- Local Fundraising: Increase local fundraising efforts through community events and partnerships with local businesses.

5. Monitor and Evaluate Progress

Key Actions:

- Regular Reporting: Maintain regular reporting on project progress, financial status, and impact.
- Impact Assessment: Conduct thorough impact assessments to measure the effectiveness and benefits of the projects.
- Adjust Strategies: Adjust strategies and plans based on the findings from monitoring and evaluations.

Summary Timeline for Year 2

Quarter | Key Activities

- Q1: Expand project implementations, recruit, and train fresh staff.
- Q2: Strengthen operational capacity, enhance donor engagement.
- Q3: Secure additional funding, monitor and evaluate progress.
- Q4: Adjust strategies, prepare for further expansion in Year 3.

Year 3: Consolidating Growth

1. Complete Ongoing Projects

Key Actions:

- Supermarket Chain: Complete construction and set-up for the remaining supermarkets.
- Hotel Chain: Finish construction for the ongoing hotel projects.
- Retail Shops: Launch the remaining retail shops.

- Apartment Buildings: Finalise construction for all apartment buildings.
- Logistics Centres: Set up the remaining logistics, storage, and distribution centres.
- Libraries: Establish the remaining libraries.
- Swimming Pools: Construct the remaining swimming pools.
- Cultural Infrastructure: Complete the development of all cultural infrastructure projects.
- Electric Bus Transportation: Implement all planned bus routes.
- Car Parks: Develop the remaining car parks.

2. Optimise Operations

Key Actions:

- Operational Reviews: Conduct thorough reviews of all operational processes and identify areas for improvement.
- Efficiency Improvements: Implement efficiency improvements across all project components to optimise performance.
- Staff Training: Provide ongoing training and development opportunities for staff to enhance their skills and capabilities.

3. Strengthen Financial Sustainability

Key Actions:

- Revenue Optimisation: Identify and implement strategies to maximise revenue from income-generating project components.
- Cost Control: Continue to monitor and control costs to ensure financial sustainability.
- Financial Reserves: Build financial reserves to ensure stability and cover unforeseen expenses.

4. Deepen Community Engagement

Key Actions:

- Community Programmes: Develop and implement community programmes to increase local involvement and support.
- Feedback Mechanisms: Establish feedback mechanisms to gather input from community members and stakeholders.
- Partnerships: Strengthen partnerships with local organisations, businesses, and government entities.

5. Prepare for Long-Term Sustainability

Key Actions:

- Long-Term Planning: Develop long-term plans for the sustainability and growth of the initiative.
- Succession Planning: Establish succession plans to ensure continuity of leadership and operations.
- Strategic Goals: Set strategic goals for the next 5-10 years to guide the future direction of the initiative.

Summary Timeline for Year 3

Quarter | Key Activities

- Q1: Complete ongoing projects, optimise operations.
- Q2: Strengthen financial sustainability, deepen community engagement.
- Q3: Prepare for long-term sustainability, set strategic goals.
- Q4: Review and consolidate growth, plan for Year 4.

Years 2 and 3 are critical for building the infrastructure and consolidating the growth of the "GiveBack to Algeria" initiative. By expanding project implementation, strengthening operational capacity, securing additional funding, and engaging the community, the initiative can achieve its goals and ensure long-term sustainability.

Years 4-5: Expansion & Sustainability for GiveBack to Algeria Initiative

In Years 4 and 5, the focus will be on expanding the initiative further, ensuring the sustainability of all projects, and solidifying the foundation laid in the previous years. These years will emphasise optimising operations, scaling successful projects, and enhancing the overall impact.

Year 4: Expansion and Optimisation

1. Scale Successful Projects

Key Actions:

- Supermarket Chain: Open an additional twenty-five supermarkets, making a total of one hundred supermarkets.
- Hotel Chain: Complete construction and open ten more hotels, bringing the total to thirty.
- Retail Shops: Launch fifty more retail shops, reaching a total of 150 shops.
- Apartment Buildings: Construct twenty-five additional apartment buildings, totalling seventy-five buildings.
- Logistics Centres: Establish five more logistics centres, totalling fifteen centres.
- Libraries: Open one hundred more libraries, achieving a total of three hundred libraries.
- Swimming Pools: Build one hundred additional swimming pools, totalling three hundred pools.
- Cultural Infrastructure: Develop twenty more cultural infrastructure projects, totalling sixty.
- Electric Bus Transportation: Implement five more bus routes, reaching twenty routes.
- Car Parks: Develop twenty-five more car parks, reaching a total of seventy-five.

2. Optimise Operational Efficiency

Key Actions:

- Operational Audits: Conduct comprehensive operational audits to identify inefficiencies and areas for improvement.

- Best Practices: Implement best practices and standardise processes across all projects.
- Technology Integration: Further integrate technology to streamline operations and enhance productivity.

3. Strengthen Financial Management

Key Actions:

- Revenue Generation: Enhance revenue generation strategies for income-generating projects.
- Cost Management: Continue rigorous cost management to ensure financial health.
- Financial Planning: Refine financial plans and forecasts to account for expanded operations.

4. Deepen Donor and Community Engagement

Key Actions:

- Engagement Programmes: Launch new donor and community engagement programmes to foster stronger relationships.
- Transparency: Increase transparency in financial reporting and project updates to build trust.
- Community Involvement: Encourage community involvement in project planning and implementation.

5. Monitor and Evaluate Impact

Key Actions:

- Impact Studies: Conduct detailed impact studies to assess the social and economic benefits of the projects.
- Feedback Mechanisms: Strengthen feedback mechanisms to gather input from beneficiaries and stakeholders.
- Adjust Strategies: Use findings from impact studies to adjust strategies and improve project outcomes.

Summary Timeline for Year 4

Quarter | Key Activities

- Q1: Scale successful projects, conduct operational audits.
- Q2: Implement best practices, enhance revenue generation.
- Q3: Deepen donor and community engagement, increase transparency.
- Q4: Conduct impact studies, adjust strategies based on findings.

Year 5: Ensuring Sustainability

1. Solidify Project Sustainability

Key Actions:

- Long-Term Contracts: Secure long-term contracts with suppliers and partners to ensure stable operations.
- Maintenance Plans: Develop comprehensive maintenance plans for all infrastructure to ensure longevity.
- Sustainability Programmes: Implement sustainability programmes to reduce environmental impact and operational costs.

2. Expand to New Regions

Key Actions:

- Market Analysis: Conduct market analysis to identify new regions for expansion.
- Pilot Projects: Launch pilot projects in new regions to assess feasibility and impact.
- Full-Scale Implementation: Roll out full-scale projects in successful pilot regions.

3. Enhance Revenue Streams

Key Actions:

- Diversify Revenue: Explore new revenue streams, such as online sales for retail shops and premium services for hotels.
- Membership Programmes: Introduce membership programmes for recurring revenue from supermarkets, pools, and libraries.
- Partnerships: Develop partnerships with local businesses for co-branding and joint ventures.

4. Institutionalise Best Practices

Key Actions:

- Standard Operating Procedures: Develop and institutionalise SOPs for all operations.
- Training Programmes: Regularly train staff on best practices and new procedures.
- Continuous Improvement: Foster a culture of continuous improvement through regular feedback and innovation.

5. Strategic Long-Term Planning

Key Actions:

- Vision and Goals: Refine the long-term vision and goals for the next 5-10 years.
- Succession Planning: Establish a succession plan to ensure leadership continuity.
- Legacy Projects: Identify and develop legacy projects that will have a lasting impact on communities.

Summary Timeline for Year 5

Quarter | Key Activities

- Q1: Solidify project sustainability, secure long-term contracts.
- Q2: Expand to new regions, launch pilot projects.
- Q3: Enhance revenue streams, introduce membership programmes.
- Q4: Institutionalise best practices, develop strategic long-term plans.

92

Years 4 and 5 focus on expanding the "GiveBack to Algeria" initiative, optimising operations, ensuring sustainability, and preparing for long-term impact. By scaling successful projects, solidifying financial health, enhancing community engagement, and strategically planning for the future, the initiative can achieve its goals and create lasting benefits for Algeria.

Years 6-7: Innovation & Consolidation for GiveBack to Algeria Initiative

In Years 6 and 7, the initiative will pivot towards innovation and consolidation. The focus will be on introducing innovative projects, further improving operational efficiency, and consolidating all efforts from previous years. These years will emphasise reinforcing the existing foundation, promoting sustainable growth, and enhancing the initiative's overall impact.

Year 6: Innovation and Growth

1. Launch Innovative Projects

Key Actions:

- Green Technology Projects: Introduce renewable energy projects such as solar farms and wind turbines to promote environmental sustainability.
- Smart Infrastructure: Implement innovative city technologies in existing and new projects to enhance efficiency and improve the quality of life.
- Educational Technology: Integrate advanced educational technology in libraries and schools to improve learning outcomes.

2. Enhance Existing Projects

Key Actions:

- Upgrade Facilities: Upgrade existing supermarkets, hotels, retail shops, and apartment buildings to meet higher standards and increase customer satisfaction.
- Expand Logistics: Increase the capacity of logistics centres to support expanded operations and ensure smooth supply chain management.

- Cultural Programmes: Develop and host new cultural programmes in the established cultural infrastructure to promote local heritage and arts.

3. Strengthen Community Engagement

Key Actions:

- Community Development Programmes: Launch new community development programmes focused on health, education, and employment.
- Volunteer Programmes: Establish volunteer programmes to involve more community members and increase grassroots support.

4. Optimise Financial Strategies

Key Actions:

- Investment Strategies: Develop and implement new investment strategies to maximise returns and ensure financial sustainability.
- Cost Reduction: Identify and execute further cost reduction strategies without compromising the quality of services.
- Financial Education: Provide financial education and support to local communities to promote economic self-sufficiency.

5. Monitor and Evaluate Progress

Key Actions:

- Advanced Impact Studies: Conduct advanced impact studies to measure the effectiveness and outcomes of innovative projects.
- Real-time Monitoring: Implement real-time monitoring systems for ongoing projects to ensure timely interventions and adjustments.
- Stakeholder Feedback: Regularly gather and analyse feedback from stakeholders to continuously improve project implementation.

Summary Timeline for Year 6

Quarter | Key Activities

- Q1: Launch innovative projects, upgrade existing facilities.
- Q2: Enhance logistics, develop cultural programmes.
- Q3: Strengthen community engagement, establish volunteer programmes.
- Q4: Optimise financial strategies, conduct advanced impact studies.

Year 7: Consolidation and Sustainability

1. Consolidate Achievements

Key Actions:

- Review Projects: Conduct a comprehensive review of all projects to ensure alignment with long-term goals.
- Standardise Procedures: Fully standardise procedures across all projects to maintain consistency and efficiency.
- Capacity Building: Invest in capacity building for staff and community members to sustain project impacts.

2. Deepen Sustainability Efforts

Key Actions:

- Sustainable Practices: Implement and reinforce sustainable practices across all operations to minimise environmental impact.
- Resource Management: Develop advanced resource management strategies to optimise the use of natural and financial resources.
- Sustainability Training: Provide ongoing training in sustainability practices for staff and community leaders.

3. Expand Successful Initiatives

Key Actions:

- Replication of Success: Identify and replicate the most successful initiatives in new areas to expand their impact.

- Pilot to Full Scale: Transition successful pilot projects from Year 6 into full-scale implementations.
- Strategic Partnerships: Form strategic partnerships with governments and private sector entities to support expansion.

4. Long-Term Financial Planning

Key Actions:

- Endowment Funds: Establish endowment funds to secure long-term financial stability.
- Revenue Diversification: Further diversify revenue streams to reduce dependency on any single source.
- Financial Risk Management: Develop and implement comprehensive financial risk management strategies.

5. Foster Innovation Culture

Key Actions:

- Innovation Hubs: Create innovation hubs to encourage creative solutions and continuous improvement.
- Incubation Programmes: Launch incubation programmes to support local entrepreneurs and startups.
- Technology Integration: Integrate innovative technology to stay ahead of industry trends and enhance service delivery.

Summary Timeline for Year 7

Quarter | Key Activities

- Q1: Review projects, standardise procedures.
- Q2: Deepen sustainability efforts, implement resource management strategies.
- Q3: Expand successful initiatives, transition pilot projects to full scale.
- Q4: Long-term financial planning, foster innovation culture

Years 6 and 7 of the "GiveBack to Algeria" initiative will focus on innovation, consolidation, and sustainability. By introducing innovative projects, enhancing existing ones, strengthening community engagement, and ensuring long-term financial stability, the initiative will be well-positioned to create lasting, impactful change in Algeria. The emphasis on continuous improvement, strategic expansion, and fostering a culture of innovation will ensure that the initiative remains dynamic and effective in addressing the needs of the Algerian communities.

Call to Action

If you have reached this part of the book, you already understand the core idea: development becomes possible when trust, structure, and collective effort come together. The next step is turning this concept into a legally compliant, professionally governed reality.

What we are asking for now (pre-registration):
• Share the initiative with your networks and invite constructive discussion.
• Help us build the founding team (governance, legal, finance, project design, communications).
• Suggest priority needs in your wilaya and identify credible local partners and experts.
• Use the hashtag #GiveBacktoAlgeria so people can find reliable information and updates.

What we will ask once the initiative is formally launched:
• A simple, accessible monthly reference contribution (illustratively €25/month), tracked transparently.
• Volunteering your time and expertise to strengthen oversight and delivery.
• Ethical sponsorship or support from organisations, only where legally permitted and under strict governance safeguards.

Stay connected:
• Website: givebacktoalgeria.com
• Email: info@givebacktoalgeria.com

Together, we can move from good intentions to durable institutions—and from institutions to tangible results across all 69 wilayas.

Future Projects Planned by the GiveBack to Algeria Initiative

The GiveBack to Algeria initiative is planning a series of future projects to overcome challenges and leverage opportunities across various sectors. These projects include transformative efforts in agriculture, the promotion of Algerian online content, the introduction of restaurant chains, the establishment of an education excellence league, a sports sponsorship initiative, investment in the fishing sector, and the development of a sustainable red meat supply chain.

Agriculture

The GiveBack to Algeria initiative plans to address the challenges and harness the opportunities within the Algerian agriculture sector through a comprehensive and multifaceted approach:

Modernisation and Technological Advancement

We will prioritise modernising agricultural practices by introducing innovative technologies, including precision farming, drip irrigation systems, and greenhouse cultivation. These innovations will enhance resource efficiency, increase crop yields, and reduce water consumption. Additionally, we will focus on developing drought-resistant crop varieties and promoting climate-smart agricultural practices to improve resilience to climate change and water scarcity. Farmers will receive training and technical assistance to enhance their knowledge and skills in modern farming techniques and sustainable land management.

Strengthening Agricultural Value Chains

Our plans include strengthening agricultural value chains by investing in post-harvest infrastructure, including advanced storage facilities, processing plants, and robust transportation networks. This will minimise post-harvest losses and ensure the timely delivery of fresh produce to markets. We also plan to establish a chain of supermarkets and an extensive storage and distribution network, ensuring efficient delivery and high-quality produce for consumers. By fostering partnerships between farmers and agribusinesses, we will create stable market outlets and ensure fair prices for agricultural products. Additionally, promoting the processing of farm products into higher-value goods will generate additional income for farmers and create new job opportunities.

Promotion of Sustainable Agricultural Practices

We will encourage organic farming practices to improve soil health and reduce reliance on chemical inputs. Investments will be made in efficient irrigation systems and water harvesting techniques to conserve water resources and promote sustainable water use. Climate-smart agricultural practices, such as agroforestry and conservation tillage, will be implemented to mitigate the impacts of climate change and enhance the resilience of farming systems.

Support for Smallholder Farmers

Supporting smallholder farmers is crucial. We will provide access to credit and financial services, enabling them to invest in their farms, adopt innovative technologies, and expand production. The initiative will support the formation and strengthening of agricultural cooperatives to empower smallholder farmers, improve their bargaining power, and facilitate better market access. Ensuring land tenure security for smallholder farmers will be a priority, incentivising investment and long-term planning to increase productivity.

Policy Reforms and Incentives

We will pursue policy reforms to streamline regulations, reduce bureaucratic hurdles, and create a more conducive environment for agricultural investment. We will advocate for tax incentives and subsidies to support investments in modern farming technologies and sustainable practices, to attract private-sector participation. Facilitating public-private partnerships will leverage the expertise and resources of both sectors, driving innovation and growth in agriculture.

Conclusion

By implementing these strategic projects, the GiveBack to Algeria initiative aims to transform Algeria's agricultural sector into a dynamic, sustainable engine of growth. These efforts will not only improve livelihoods but also ensure food security for the country. The integration of a supermarket chain and a robust storage and distribution network will play a critical role in maintaining the supply chain, reducing waste, and ensuring that high-quality agricultural products are available to consumers.

Red Meat Supply

Introduction

To ensure a sustainable and reliable supply of red meat for the GiveBack to Algeria initiative, focusing exclusively on local production, the following steps will be taken:

1. Establish Direct Relationships with Local Farmers

Direct Procurement:

o   Partnerships with Local Farmers: We plan to build strong relationships with sheep and cattle farmers through cooperatives or direct agreements, ensuring a steady supply of meat while supporting local agriculture.

o   Contracts and Agreements: Create long-term contracts with farmers to ensure a consistent supply of meat and provide financial stability to the farmers.

Support and Investment:

o   Training and Development: Invest in training programmes for farmers on sustainable and efficient farming practices, including animal health management and modern breeding techniques.

o   Financial Assistance: Provide financial support or microloans to farmers for purchasing livestock, improving farm infrastructure, and accessing better feed and veterinary services.

2. Develop Processing and Distribution Infrastructure

Processing Facilities:

o   Local Slaughterhouses and Processing Plants: Invest in or partner with local slaughterhouses and meat processing facilities to ensure hygienic and efficient meat processing, maintaining high quality and safety standards.

Cold Chain Logistics:

o   Refrigeration and Transportation: Develop a robust cold chain logistics system, including refrigerated transportation and storage facilities, to maintain the freshness and quality of the meat from farm to supermarket or restaurant.

3. Implement Quality Assurance Programmes

Certification and Standards:

o   Quality Control: Implement strict quality control measures and certification programmes to ensure the meat supplied meets health and safety standards.

o   Traceability Systems: Develop traceability systems to track the origin of the meat, ensuring transparency and building consumer trust.

4. Foster Cooperative Models

Cooperative Farming:

o   Form Cooperatives: Encourage farmers to form cooperatives to pool resources, share knowledge, and improve bargaining power. Cooperatives can also help in bulk purchasing of feed and veterinary services, reducing costs.

Community Support:

o   Community Engagement: Engage local communities in the initiative to foster a sense of ownership and responsibility towards sustainable livestock farming practices.

5. Invest in Marketing and Consumer Education

Promotion of Local Products:

o   Branding and Marketing: Promote the locally sourced meat through branding and marketing campaigns that highlight the benefits of supporting local farmers and the superior quality of the product.

o   Consumer Education: Educate consumers about the importance of supporting local agriculture and the nutritional benefits of locally sourced meat.

6. Collaborate with Government and Industry Stakeholders

Policy and Advocacy:

o   Government Support: Work with government agencies to access subsidies, grants, and other forms of support for the agriculture sector. Advocate for policies that support sustainable livestock farming and local meat production.

o   Industry Associations: Collaborate with industry associations and participate in trade fairs and exhibitions to stay informed about market trends and innovations in the meat industry.

7. Focus on Sustainability and Innovation

Sustainable Practices:

o   Eco-friendly Farming: Encourage and support sustainable farming practices that minimise environmental impact, such as rotational grazing and organic farming methods.

o   Innovation and Technology: Invest in innovative technologies like hydroponic feed production and genetic improvements to enhance meat production efficiency and quality.

8. Develop Local Feed Production

Self-sufficiency in Feed:

> o   Feed Production: Invest in local feed production to ensure a stable supply of quality feed for livestock. This includes cultivating feed crops and producing high-quality cattle and sheep feed.
> o   Feed Quality Control: Implement standards and quality control measures for feed production to ensure nutritional adequacy and safety for livestock.

By implementing these strategies, the GiveBack to Algeria initiative can create a reliable, high-quality, and sustainable red meat supply chain that benefits local farmers, meets consumer demand, and supports Algeria's overall economic development. This approach will not only ensure food security but also promote regional economic growth and agricultural sector sustainability.

Fish & Fishing

Introduction

To invest effectively in the fishing sector and secure a steady supply of fish for the GiveBack to Algeria initiative chain of supermarkets, hotels, and future restaurants, several strategic steps will be taken:

1.   Investment in Aquaculture

Aquaculture Development:

> o   Establish Aquaculture Farms: We plan to invest in the development of aquaculture farms to ensure a consistent supply of various fish species. This includes both inland and coastal aquaculture.
> o   Training and Support: Provide training programmes for local farmers on modern aquaculture techniques to increase productivity and sustainability.

Benefits:

o   Ensures a stable supply of fish regardless of seasonal fluctuations.

o   Reduces pressure on wild fish stocks and promotes sustainable fishing practices.

2.   Partnerships and Collaboration

Collaborate with Local Fishermen:

o   Cooperatives and Associations: We will form cooperatives or associations with local fishers to ensure fair trade practices and a steady supply chain.

o   Direct Procurement: Establish direct procurement agreements with fishing communities to secure a steady and reliable supply of fish.

Benefits:

o   Supports local economies and communities.

o   Provides a stable and potentially lower-cost supply chain for the GiveBack initiative.

3.   Infrastructure Investment

Cold Chain Development:

o   Cold Storage Facilities: Invest in cold storage facilities near fishing areas to preserve the freshness and quality of fish.

o   Logistics and Transportation: Develop efficient logistics and transportation networks to quickly move fish from catch points to retail and hotel locations.

Benefits:

o   Reduces spoilage and ensures a high-quality fish supply.

o   Enhances the ability to distribute fish across various retail and hospitality locations.

4.   **Sustainable Practices**

Sustainability Certification:

o   Eco-Certifications: Encourage and support local fishers and aquaculture farms to obtain eco-certifications such as MSC (Marine Stewardship Council) or ASC (Aquaculture Stewardship Council).

o   Sustainable Practices: Implement and promote sustainable fishing and farming practices to ensure the long-term viability of fish stocks.

Benefits:

o   Aligns with global sustainability goals and enhances the brand reputation of GiveBack.

o   Ensures long-term availability of fish resources.

5.   Research and Development

R&D Investment:

o   Innovative Techniques: Invest in research and development to discover innovative techniques in fish farming and sustainable fishing.

o   Technology Adoption: Encourage the adoption of technology in monitoring fish health, water quality, and efficient feed management.

Benefits:

o   Increases productivity and efficiency in fish production.

o   Reduces environmental impact and promotes sustainable growth.

6.   Market and Value Chain Development

Market Expansion:

o   Export Potential: Explore opportunities for exporting high-quality fish to international markets to increase revenue.

o   Product Diversification: Develop a variety of fish products (e.g., fillets, smoked fish, canned fish) to cater to different market segments.

Benefits:

o   Diversifies revenue streams and reduces dependency on a single market.
o   Enhances brand presence and market reach.

Implementation Strategy

- Feasibility Studies: Conduct feasibility studies to identify the best locations for aquaculture farms and cold storage facilities.
- Stakeholder Engagement: Engage with local communities, government bodies, and industry experts to align the investment strategy with local needs and regulatory requirements.
- Pilot Projects: Initiate pilot projects to assess and refine aquaculture techniques and supply chain logistics before scaling up.
- Monitoring and Evaluation: Implement robust monitoring and evaluation frameworks to track progress and make necessary adjustments.

By investing in aquaculture, building strong partnerships, enhancing infrastructure, promoting sustainability, and fostering research and development, GiveBack to Algeria can secure a reliable and high-quality supply of fish for its supermarkets, hotels, and future restaurants. This approach not only ensures food security but also supports local economies and promotes sustainable practices.

GiveBack to Algeria Restaurant Chains

Introduction

As part of future initiatives under the GiveBack to Algeria programme, we plan to develop two groundbreaking projects: a chain of fast-food restaurants and a chain of fine-dining restaurants across Algeria. These ventures are designed to boost economic growth, generate employment opportunities, and enhance Algeria's culinary landscape.

Project Goals

- Economic Development: To contribute to Algeria's economic growth by creating jobs and supporting local suppliers.
- Culinary Excellence: To offer high-quality food options, ranging from quick, affordable meals to exquisite fine dining experiences.
- Community Engagement: To engage with local communities and foster a culture of giving back through sustainable practices and local sourcing.

Fast Food Restaurant Chain: "Quick Bites"

- Business Concept: "Quick Bites" will offer a diverse menu of affordable, fast, and delicious meals catering to a broad audience. The chain will emphasise speed, convenience, and consistency while maintaining lofty standards of quality and hygiene.
- Target Market:
  - Young professionals and students
  - Families seeking quick meal options.
  - Tourists looking for local flavours in a convenient format.
- Menu Highlights:
  - Local favourites such as shawarma, couscous, and merguez sandwiches
  - International fast-food items like burgers, fries, and wraps
  - Healthy options including salads and fresh juices.
- Locations: Major cities such as Algiers, Oran, and Constantine; High-traffic areas like shopping malls, business districts, and transportation hubs

Importance of Creating a Fast-Food Chain

The fast-food industry is crucial in providing quick, affordable meal options for busy urban populations. In Algeria, where demand for convenient dining solutions is growing, a chain like "Quick Bites" can fill a significant market gap. Moreover, the fast-food industry can create numerous employment opportunities, particularly for young people and students, and support local agriculture by sourcing ingredients locally.

Fine Dining Restaurant Chain: "Elégance"

- Business Concept: "Elégance" will provide a luxurious dining experience, showcasing the rich culinary heritage of Algeria with a modern twist. The chain will focus on exceptional service, elegant ambience, and gourmet cuisine.
  - Target Market:
    - Affluent locals and expatriates
    - Business executives and professionals
    - Tourists seeking a high-end dining experience.
  - Menu Highlights:
    - Gourmet interpretations of traditional Algerian dishes
    - Extensive beverage list featuring local and international selections.
    - Seasonal and locally sourced ingredients
  - Locations: Prime locations in major cities such as Algiers, Oran, and Constantine; High-end neighbourhoods and business districts

Importance of Creating a Fine Dining Chain

Fine dining establishments play a critical role in highlighting and preserving culinary traditions while introducing innovative culinary techniques. "Elégance" aims to elevate Algerian cuisine to international standards, attracting both local and international clientele. These restaurants will not only create direct employment opportunities but also promote tourism and the hospitality sector. Additionally, they will foster local pride and global recognition of Algerian culinary arts.

The planned "GiveBack to Algeria" restaurant chains—"Quick Bites" and "Elégance"—are set to impact the country's culinary scene and economy significantly. By offering diverse dining experiences and creating numerous job opportunities, these ventures will contribute to the broader goal of sustainable economic development in Algeria. The success of these projects will be measured not only in financial terms but also by their positive impact on the community and local industry.

Education Excellence League (EEL)

Part of the GiveBack to Algeria Initiative

Project Overview

Name: Education Excellence League (EEL)

Objective: To promote academic excellence, sportsmanship, and extracurricular activities through friendly competitions and league tables among primary schools, secondary schools, and universities in Algeria.

Key Components

1. League Tables
   - Categories:
     - Primary Schools
     - Secondary Schools
     - Universities
   - Criteria:
     - Academic performance (standardised test scores, grades)
     - Sports achievements (regional and national competition results)
     - Extracurricular activities (clubs, arts, music)
     - Community service (volunteer hours, impact projects)
     - Innovation projects (science fairs, tech competitions)
   - Scoring System:
     - Points awarded based on performance in each category.
     - Regular updates and publications of league standings to maintain a competitive spirit.
2. Competitions
   - Weekly Competitions:
     - Subjects: Mathematics, Science, Literature, History, etc.
     - Format: Quizzes, debates, science fairs, talent shows

o   Sports Competitions: Football, basketball, athletics, and other popular sports.

o   Extracurricular Activities: Art, music, drama, and community service projects.

3. Televised Events

o   Weekly Broadcasts: Highlights of the competitions, featuring interviews, performances, and award ceremonies.

o   Educational Programmes: Segments on various educational topics, featuring guest speakers and educational content.

o   Partnerships: Collaborations with local TV channels and online streaming platforms to reach a wider audience.

4. Awards and Recognition

o   Monthly and Yearly Awards: Trophies, certificates, and scholarships for top performers in each category.

o   Special Recognitions: For innovation, community service, and outstanding sportsmanship.

5. **Community Engagement**

o   Parental Involvement: Encouraging parents to participate and support their children's activities.

o   Local Businesses: Partnering with businesses for sponsorships and prizes.

o   Volunteers: Involving local volunteers for event organisation and mentoring.

Implementation Plan

1. Planning and Organisation

o   Form Committees: Establish committees for each category (academic, sports, extracurricular) to plan and oversee competitions.

o   Partnerships: Establish partnerships with educational institutions, media houses, and sponsors.

2. Pilot Programme

o   Select Schools and Universities: Start with a few institutions to pilot the programme and refine the process.

o   Initial Competitions: Conduct initial rounds of competitions and televised events.

3. Full-Scale Launch

o   Expand Participation: Invite more schools and universities to join the league.

o   Regular Updates: Maintain league tables and organise regular competitions.

o   Continuous Improvement: Gather feedback and continuously improve the programme.

4. Sustainability

o   Funding: Secure funding through sponsorships, government grants, and community donations.

o   Publicity: Use social media, local newspapers, and community events to promote the initiative.

o   Impact Assessment: Regularly assess the impact of the programme on students' academic performance, personal development, and community involvement.

Benefits

- Academic Excellence: Encourages students to excel academically through healthy competition.
- Skill Development: Promotes sportsmanship, creativity, and leadership skills.
- Community Spirit: Fosters a sense of community and collaboration among students, parents, and educators.
- National Pride: Highlights the talents and achievements of Algerian students on a national platform.

Additional Details

- Example Competitions:

o   Academic Quizzes: Weekly themed quizzes for different subjects, broadcast live.

o   Science Fairs: Monthly fairs showcasing student projects with expert judges.

o   Sports Tournaments: Seasonal tournaments for football, basketball, and athletics.

o   Art and Music Festivals: Annual festivals celebrating student talent in the arts.

- Example Awards:
    o Best School/University of the Month: Based on overall performance in all categories.
    o Top Innovator Award: For the most innovative science/tech project.
    o Community Hero Award: For outstanding contributions to community service.

Monitoring and Evaluation

- Feedback Surveys: Regular surveys from students, teachers, and parents.
- Performance Analytics: Data analysis to track performance trends and impact.
- Advisory Board: A board of educators and experts to provide ongoing guidance and oversight.

By implementing the Education Excellence League as part of the GiveBack to Algeria initiative, we aim to foster a culture of excellence and continuous improvement in Algeria's education system, providing students with numerous opportunities to shine and develop both academically and personally.

Sports Sponsorship Initiative Strategy

Introduction

Objective: To support and nurture young Algerian sports talents by providing comprehensive assistance to help them succeed in their chosen sports, fostering future professional athletes and champions.

1. Need and Purpose of the Initiative

1.1. Addressing the Youth Demographic and Potential

Algeria boasts a youthful population, with approximately 54% of its citizens under 30. This demographic has significant potential for the nation across various fields, particularly in sports. Young people possess the vigour, enthusiasm, and adaptability required to excel in athletics. However, despite this potential, many young Algerian athletes face substantial challenges in accessing quality training, facilities, and financial support.

1.2. Nurturing Future Champions

The primary purpose of the GiveBack to Algeria Sports Sponsorship Initiative is to bridge this gap by providing young athletes with the resources and opportunities they need to excel. By focusing on early identification and support, we aim to nurture future champions who can represent Algeria on the global stage. This initiative is designed to ensure that promising talents receive the coaching, training, and support they need to reach their full potential.

1.3. Enhancing National Representation in International Sports

Historically, Algeria has produced exceptional athletes who have made their mark in international sports events. From the legendary runner Noureddine Morceli to football star Riyad Mahrez, Algerian athletes have demonstrated the country's potential on the world stage. However, the journey to international success is fraught with obstacles, and many talented individuals lack the means to pursue their dreams. The GiveBack to Algeria initiative aims to change this by creating a structured pathway for young athletes and enhancing Algeria's representation at international sports events.

1.4. Socio-Economic Impact

Investing in sports development has far-reaching socio-economic benefits. It promotes physical health, instils discipline, and provides positive role models for the youth. Additionally, successful athletes can inspire national pride and unity, and their achievements can elevate Algeria's profile on the international stage. By fostering a culture of sports excellence, we can contribute to the holistic development of our youth, steering them away from negative influences and providing them with opportunities for personal and professional growth.

2. Programme Structure and Governance

2.1. Establish a Steering Committee

o   Composition: Include former athletes, sports professionals, educators, and business leaders.
o   Responsibilities: Oversee the programme, make strategic decisions, and ensure alignment with overall objectives.

2.2. Create Regional Coordinators

o   Role: Manage local implementation of the initiative, consult with schools, sports clubs, and communities.

3.   Talent Identification and Recruitment

3.1. School and Community Outreach

o   Activities: Organise sports days, competitions, and workshops in schools and communities to identify talent.
o   Partnerships: Collaborate with schools, local sports clubs, and community organisations to reach a wider pool of potential athletes.

3.2. Talent Scouting Programmes

o   Scouting Events: Regularly hold scouting events and trials across different regions.
o   Evaluation Criteria: Develop a standardised evaluation system to assess potential based on physical, technical, and psychological attributes.

4.   Support Framework

4.1. Training and Coaching

o   Facilities: Provide access to high-quality training facilities and equipment.
o   Coaching Staff: Employ experienced coaches and trainers in various sports disciplines.

o Development Programmes: Design personalised development programmes tailored to the needs of each athlete.

4.2. Financial Support

o Scholarships: Offer scholarships to cover training, equipment, travel, and competition expenses.
o Grants: Provide grants for advanced training camps and international exposure.

4.3. Academic Support

o Education Plans: Develop education plans that allow athletes to balance their sports and academic commitments.
o Tutoring Services: Offer tutoring and academic support to ensure athletes do not fall behind in their studies.

5. Health and Well-being

5.1. Medical Support

o Healthcare Access: Ensure access to regular health check-ups, physiotherapy, and sports medicine.
o Nutrition Plans: Develop individualised nutrition plans to optimise performance and recovery.

5.2. Mental Health Support

o Counselling Services: Provide access to sports psychologists and mental health professionals.
o Workshops: Conduct workshops on mental resilience, stress management, and coping strategies.

6. Performance Monitoring and Evaluation

6.1. Tracking Progress

o Metrics: Establish key performance indicators (KPIs) to track athletes' progress.

o   Regular Assessments: Conduct regular performance assessments and adjust training programmes as needed.

6.2. Feedback Mechanisms

o   Feedback Sessions: Hold periodic feedback sessions with athletes and coaches.
o   Improvement Plans: Develop and implement improvement plans based on feedback.

7.   Partnerships and Sponsorships

7.1. Corporate Sponsorships

o   Sponsorship Packages: Create attractive sponsorship packages for businesses to support athletes.
o   Brand Alignment: Ensure sponsors' values align with the initiative's goals.

7.2. Government and NGO Partnerships

o   Collaborations: Partner with government bodies and NGOs for additional support and resources.
o   Funding: Seek grants and funding opportunities from various sources.

8.   Promotion and Community Engagement

8.1. Marketing and PR Campaigns

o   Campaigns: Develop marketing and PR campaigns to raise awareness about the initiative.
o   Success Stories: Highlight success stories of sponsored athletes to inspire and attract more participants.

8.2. Community Involvement

o   Volunteer Programmes: Encourage community members to volunteer and support local talents.

o   Engagement Events: Organise events that bring together athletes, families, and communities.

9. Sustainability and Future Growth

9.1. Long-term Planning

o   Vision: Develop a long-term vision for the initiative with clear milestones and objectives.

o   Scalability: Create a scalable model that can be expanded to include more athletes and sports disciplines.

9.2. Continuous Improvement

o   Feedback Loops: Implement continuous feedback loops to identify areas for improvement.

o   Innovation: Stay updated with the latest trends and innovations in sports development and incorporate them into the programme.

Implementation Timeline

Year 1: Foundation and Pilot Phase

- Establish the steering committee and regional coordinators.
- Launch school and community outreach programmes.
- Initiate pilot scouting and training programmes in selected regions.

Year 2-3: Expansion and Consolidation

- Expand the initiative to more regions.
- Develop partnerships with more schools, clubs, and sponsors.
- Refine and scale up training, financial, and academic support programmes.

Year 4-5: Full Scale Operation

- Fully operationalise the programme across the country.

- Continuously monitor, evaluate, and improve the initiative.
- Build a strong pipeline of future professional athletes and champions.

This strategy aims to create a robust framework to identify, support, and develop young sports talents in Algeria, ensuring they have the resources and guidance needed to excel in their chosen fields. By addressing the needs of the young population and leveraging their potential, we can enhance Algeria's presence in international sports, contributing to national pride and socio-economic development.

Algerian Online Content

Detailed Proposal: Creation of an Online Content Team for Promoting Algerian History and Culture

Introduction

The rich history and diverse culture of Algeria are treasures that deserve to be widely shared and celebrated. With the advent of digital media, there is a unique opportunity to create a suite of websites that serve as comprehensive repositories of Algerian history, culture, and achievements. These websites will cater to both local and international audiences, providing valuable educational resources and promoting cross-cultural understanding.

Project Scope

We plan to create a series of websites, each focusing on various aspects of Algerian culture and history:

dzcinema.com

- Content: Detailed information on Algerian cinema, including filmographies, biographies of key figures in the industry, reviews, and analyses.
- Features: Searchable database, multimedia galleries, and user-generated content sections.

dztheatre.com

- Content: Information on the history of Algerian theatre, notable plays, playwrights, and contemporary theatre news.
- Features: Interactive timelines, video archives of performances, and interviews with theatre personalities.

dzhistoire.com

- Content: Comprehensive historical accounts of Algeria, key events, and influential figures.
- Features: Detailed timelines, primary source documents, and interactive maps.

dzsports.com

- Content: Coverage of various sports in Algeria, including football, handball, basketball, boxing, and judo. Biographies of athletes, records, and significant achievements.
- Features: Live score updates, athlete profiles, and historical records.

dzbiographies.com

- Content: Biographies of prominent Algerian figures from various fields such as politics, arts, science, and literature.
- Features: Searchable biographies, multimedia content, and user contributions.

01111954.com, 08051945.com, 05071962.com

- Content: Dedicated to specific significant dates in Algerian history, providing detailed narratives and archival material related to these dates.
- Features: Archival documents, eyewitness accounts, and interactive storytelling.

Team Composition

To ensure the success of this project, we will assemble a multidisciplinary team comprising the following members:

- Content Creators: Writers, editors, and multimedia specialists to produce high-quality articles, videos, and interactive content.
- Historians and Researchers: Experts in Algerian history and culture to provide accurate and in-depth information.
- University Collaborators: Partnerships with Algerian universities to facilitate academic research and provide access to educational resources.
- Archivists: Professionals skilled in managing and curating historical documents and artefacts.
- IT and Web Development Team: Designers and developers to create and maintain user-friendly, visually appealing websites.
- Marketing and Outreach Team: To promote the websites and ensure they reach a broad audience.

Implementation Plan

1. Research and Content Development
   o Collaboration: Collaborate closely with historians, researchers, and universities to gather authentic and detailed content.
   o Content Calendar: Develop a content calendar to plan and schedule the creation and publication of content.
   o Multimedia Content: Produce a variety of content formats, including articles, videos, podcasts, and infographics.
2. Website Design and Development
   o Professional Development Team: Hire a skilled web development team to design and build the websites.
   o User Experience: Focus on creating a user-friendly interface with easy navigation and search functionality.
   o Multimedia Integration: Ensure the websites can host various multimedia elements like videos, images, and interactive features.
3. Archival and Database Management
   o Partnerships: Establish partnerships with national archives, museums, and libraries.
   o Digitisation: Digitise historical documents, photographs, and other resources for online access.
   o Database Creation: Develop an organised, searchable database to store and manage digital content.

4. Marketing and Outreach
   o   Marketing Strategy: Develop a comprehensive marketing plan to promote the website.
   o   Social Media: Utilise social media platforms to reach a broad audience and engage users.
   o   Media Partnerships: Collaborate with Algerian television channels, newspapers, and other media outlets for promotional activities.
5. Continuous Improvement and Engagement
   o   Regular Updates: Keep the content fresh and relevant with regular updates and new additions.
   o   User Engagement: Foster user engagement through social media, comments, and interactive features.
   o   Feedback Mechanism: Implement a feedback system to gather user input and make continuous improvements.

Justification and Importance

- Cultural Preservation: Algeria's rich history and diverse culture are invaluable assets. These websites will play a crucial role in preserving and promoting this heritage for future generations.
- Educational Resource: The websites will serve as valuable educational tools for students, researchers, and anyone interested in Algerian history and culture.
- Global Reach: Establishing an online presence will make Algerian culture accessible to a global audience, promoting cross-cultural understanding and appreciation.
- National Pride: Highlighting the achievements and contributions of Algerian figures and events will foster a sense of national pride and identity.

Partnerships and Collaborations

- Universities: Partner with Algerian universities to involve students and faculty in research and content creation.
- Television and Media: Collaborate with Algerian television channels and other media outlets to promote the websites and content.

- Cultural Institutions: Work with museums, libraries, and cultural organisations to access resources and support promotional activities.

Budget and Funding

- Initial Investment: Estimate the costs for web development, content creation, and initial marketing efforts.
- Ongoing Costs: Budget for maintenance, content updates, and continuous marketing efforts.
- Funding Sources: Funding for these projects is secured through a multi-faceted approach, ensuring a steady and sustainable flow of resources. The primary sources of funding include:
  - GiveBack to Algeria's Income-Generating Projects: We undertake various income-generating projects that not only fund our initiatives but also provide employment and economic opportunities within the communities we serve. These projects are designed to be sustainable and impactful, creating a virtuous cycle of development and reinvestment.
  - Corporate Partnerships: Partnerships with corporations play a crucial role in our funding strategy. Businesses that share our vision for a prosperous Algeria provide substantial support through donations, sponsorships, and collaborative projects. These partnerships are mutually beneficial, enhancing corporate social responsibility while driving significant social change.

Creating dedicated websites to showcase Algerian history and culture is a vital project that will preserve and promote the nation's rich heritage. By assembling a team of talented content creators, historians, archivists, and IT professionals, and by leveraging partnerships with universities and media outlets, this project will ensure that Algeria's legacy is accessible, celebrated, and understood both locally and globally. This endeavour will not only educate and inform but also inspire pride and appreciation for Algeria's rich cultural tapestry.

Conclusion: The Imperative of the GiveBack to Algeria Initiative

The Need for the GiveBack to Algeria Initiative

Algeria, a nation rich in history, culture, and natural resources, stands at a crossroads. While its past is filled with stories of resilience and determination, its present faces significant challenges. From the remnants of colonial infrastructure to the pressing needs of a growing population, Algeria's old neighbourhoods and modern cities alike require thoughtful intervention to reach their full potential.

Urban areas, with their historical quarters, are particularly in need of revitalisation. These neighbourhoods, once vibrant centres of community life, now suffer from overcrowding, deteriorating infrastructure, and economic stagnation. The youth, our greatest asset, face limited opportunities, driving many to seek prospects abroad. Traditional food markets, a hallmark of daily life, often struggle with inefficiencies that affect producers and consumers alike. Meanwhile, the tourism sector, brimming with untapped potential, remains underdeveloped, missing the chance to showcase Algeria's rich heritage to the world.

The Idea Behind the GiveBack to Algeria Initiative

The "GiveBack to Algeria" initiative is a bold, visionary response to these challenges. It seeks to mobilise the collective power of the Algerian diaspora and local communities to transform Algeria through strategic investments in key sectors. This initiative is not merely about building physical structures; it is about fostering a culture of sustainable development, community engagement, and economic empowerment.

The initiative is multifaceted, targeting key areas including housing, retail, logistics, education, cultural preservation, transportation, and urban planning. By establishing chains of supermarkets, hotels, and shops, building modern apartment complexes, creating libraries and swimming pools in every neighbourhood, revitalising theatres and cultural spaces, and enhancing urban mobility with electric bus networks and car parks, the initiative aims to create a comprehensive framework for growth and development.

Each project is designed to address specific needs while contributing to the broader vision of a modern, prosperous, and sustainable Algeria. By focusing on direct procurement, efficient logistics, and sustainable practices, the initiative seeks to streamline processes, reduce costs, and create economic opportunities. The involvement of local communities in planning and implementation ensures that the projects are tailored to meet the unique needs and preferences of the people they serve.

The Importance of Participation and Support

The success of the "GiveBack to Algeria" initiative hinges on the active participation and support of Algerians, both at home and abroad. This is a collective endeavour, rooted in the belief that together, we can achieve far more than we could individually.

For the Algerian diaspora, this initiative offers a tangible way to contribute to the development of the homeland. It is an opportunity to invest in projects that will create lasting benefits for future generations. By contributing to the initiative, you help build a legacy of progress and hope, honouring the sacrifices of those who fought for Algeria's independence and striving to fulfil their dream of a free and prosperous nation.

For local communities, the initiative provides a platform to shape their future actively. It fosters a sense of ownership and pride, empowering residents to take charge of their neighbourhoods and work collaboratively towards common goals. The improved infrastructure, enhanced public services, and increased economic opportunities resulting from these projects will directly impact the quality of life, making Algeria a better place to live, work, and thrive.

Hand in Hand: Rebuilding and Modernising

In conclusion, the "GiveBack to Algeria" initiative is more than a series of projects; it is a movement towards a brighter future. It is a call to action for all who believe in the power of collective effort and the potential of a united community. By participating and supporting this initiative, we take significant steps towards rebuilding our old neighbourhoods, modernising our local and national economy, and creating a sustainable, prosperous future for all Algerians.

Hand in hand, we will revitalise our cities, honour our rich cultural heritage, and pave the way for future generations. Together, we can transform Algeria into a beacon of progress, demonstrating that with determination, collaboration, and a shared vision, we can achieve extraordinary things. Join us in the "GiveBack to Algeria" initiative and be a part of this transformative journey. Let us build tomorrow, today.

Toufik Bakhti
info@givebacktoalgeria.com
00447722295814
info@givebacktoalgeria.com

The "Give Back to Algeria" book is now available for purchase on Amazon! All proceeds from the sale will go directly towards covering the essential setup costs of the initiative, including website development, establishing the fund in Algeria, legal fees, and all necessary expenses to get the project off the ground. The financial details will be published monthly on the initiative's website to ensure transparency. By purchasing this book, you are playing a key role in laying the foundation for a movement that will drive Algeria's future development.

"Thank You for Reading & Sharing"

Thank you for taking the time to read this book and becoming part of the journey to a brighter future for Algeria. Your support doesn't end here. By sharing this book with others, you help spread the vision and bring us one step closer to realising the GiveBack to Algeria Initiative. Together, we can build a modern, prosperous Algeria. Let's make this dream a reality!

www.ingramcontent.com/pod-product-compliance
Lightning Source LLC
Chambersburg PA
CBHW071034250726
48653CB00005B/1844